KJV: Scripture quotations are taken from the King James Version. Public domain.

ESV: Scripture quotations are taken from the ESV® Bible (The Holy Bible, English Standard Version®). Copyright © 2001 by Crossway, a publishing ministry of Good News Publishers. Used by permission. All rights reserved.

Straight Outta Brokenness, And It Didn't Kill Me! is a work of nonfiction.

Copyright © 2024 by Candie A. Mitchell-Price. All rights reserved.

Published in the United States by Candie A. Mitchell-Price. All photos are from the author's collection.

Paperback ISBN 9798991269902
Ebook   ISBN 9798991269919
Workbook ISBN 9798991269926

candieprice.com
First Edition

STRAIGHT OUTTA BROKENNESS
AND IT DIDN'T KILL ME!

CANDIE A. MITCHELL-PRICE

ALSO BY CANDIE A. MITCHELL-PRICE

First Lady: The Real Truth,
A Practical Approach to an Ambiguous Role

He Restoreth My Soul, A Devotional

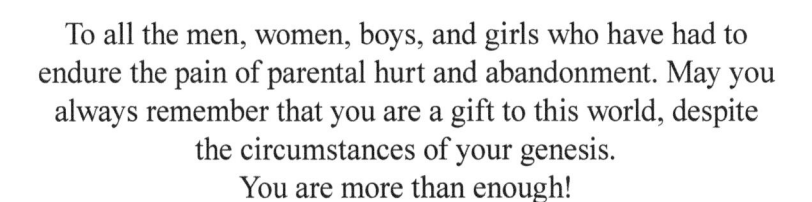

To all the men, women, boys, and girls who have had to endure the pain of parental hurt and abandonment. May you always remember that you are a gift to this world, despite the circumstances of your genesis.
You are more than enough!

FOREWARD..iv

INTRODUCTION..viii

PART 1: BROKEN PIECES...1

   CHAPTER 1: FINDING TERRY...3

   CHAPTER 2: INVISIBLE: HIDING
   IN PLAIN SIGHT 29

   CHAPTER 3: ABSENT DAD AND
   MOTHER WOUNDS..49

   CHAPTER 4: ON MY OWN FOR REAL 83

PART 2: PUZZLE PIECES..101

   CHAPTER 5: PRINCE CHARMING
   COMES ANYWAY..103

CONTENTS

CHAPTER 6: MOTHERHOOD FROM
THE MOTHERLESS..........................121

PART 3: HEALING..............................141

CHAPTER 7: FORGIVENESS IS THE
ROAD LESS TRAVELED.................143

CHAPTER 8: THE ANTWON FISHER EFFECT..........157

CHAPTER 9: FUNERALIZING LOST
RELATIONSHIPS..............................177

CHAPTER 10: STRONGER DIDN'T KILL ME............185

DEAR TERRY.....................................197

ACKNOWLEDGEMENTS..................205

"all my life I had to fight..."
it's more than just a memorable
line from a purple screen
I crawled in this world pushing, prodding,
peeping, yet purpose filled
prying my eyes open til three pounds
became more, crying til lungs grew strong
and the world knew I was here
although no one to call dad, daddy,
poppa, father, sir...
the mystery and the history of my genesis
would lurk in the shadows of my life for many years -
toiling with my emotions, telling me I'm not worthy,
trying to get me to surrender to the repercussions
which would always erect a wall between me and everyone else
....as Brother Langston hailed, "Life for me ain't been no crystal stair" -
it's been filled with broken planks and life-sized splinters
that pierce my soul…

my story. this poem. unfinished.

c/Candie A. Mitchell-Price
May 7, 2019

FOREWARD

I am April Betner, a therapist, preacher, and author and I have known Candie from a distance for over a decade. I know her to be a phenomenal speaker, gifted writer, educator, strategist, and entrepreneur. She is also a devoted wife, mother, and friend. In 2007 and 2015 (reprinted), Candie released a book titled "First Lady: The Real Truth, A Practical Approach to an Ambiguous Role." When my husband was called to pastor a church, I found myself facing challenges that I did not anticipate. Candie's book was a source of encouragement, inspiration, comfort, and education to me as I embarked on this new journey of being a pastor's wife. Her candid and straightforward delivery blessed my life. She ministered to me from a distance and didn't even know it.

In recent years, I have come to know Candie more closely. She graciously invited me into her world, her space, and her pain. I have been encouraged and inspired by her authenticity, transparency, and her resilience. I have been equally moved by her determination to move beyond her brokenness, but not from a place that buries or suppresses it, but a place that addresses it head-on. Candie has and continues to courageously confront her brokenness and in doing so, she has stripped its power to control and dominate her life.

As a mental health therapist and minister, I am very familiar with the reality of brokenness and its impact. In both arenas where I serve, whether the couch or the pulpit, I encounter individuals who have been deeply wounded. Many of these wounds have roots that run deep and can be traced back to childhood trauma. When we are hurt by those who have been trusted to love, provide, and care for us, that reality creates wounds - many of which do not heal on their own. Unresolved issues and past trauma, whether from childhood, family of origin, or previous relationships, will show up in your present and will threaten your future if you fail to deal with them. Even worse, they can potentially have a negative impact on future generations. We owe it to ourselves and those coming behind us to pursue healing and wholeness.

The phrase "time heals all wounds" is a lie. Healing takes more than time. Healing takes work! Healing takes courage. Moreover, the healing process often involves even more pain. Yet this process that can feel like pain on top of pain is not without purpose. Just when it feels like you are broken beyond repair, you may soon learn that all of those broken pieces are being divinely reconstructed by something bigger than you. Through the process, falling apart somehow morphs into a phenomenon of falling into place.

In her memoir, Straight Outta Brokeness, Candie invites you into her journey of brokenness. The beautiful thing about a memoir is that it has the potential to draw you into someone else's world and experience while simultaneously creating space for you to reflect on your own. Straight Out of Brokenness is masterful, transparent, real, raw, and riveting. Candie's personality laces every page, and you will experience her heart, her grit, her humor, her determination, and her faith as you read her story. Her book will make you laugh, cry, reflect, and ponder. Candie invites you into her pain but she won't leave you there. Her story is one of faith, triumph, victory, and hope, and it will undoubtedly inspire you no matter where you find yourself in this journey of life.

Rev. April N. Betner, LCSW, MTS

"As we heal ourselves, recognize, grieve, and release the cycles of brokenness we've inherited and often pass on, can we more patiently and gingerly handle those who are cracked and sharp around the edges?

So many of us learned to hunch ourselves in the face of rejection and negation and deprivation.

What if we straightened our spines, fixed every vertebrae? We are all worthy of restoration, of visibility, of dignity. Our humanity matters."

-Tariq Black Thought Trotter, The Upcycled Self

INTRODUCTION

"That which does not kill us, makes us stronger."
  - Friedrich Nietzsche

I'm not quite sure when I was exposed to this quote, but I feel like I've been holding it dear to my heart for most of my life, or at least subconsciously, for as long as I've been able to process pain and anything in my life that I felt was fashioned to kill me, to break me, or annihilate me. If I came out on the other side of it, I became stronger, right? Or did I? Was I really stronger or was I just able to hide my feelings about what I had endured so that I could muster enough strength to keep on going and not succumb to my wounds? As a Black woman raised in America, I, like so many Black women (and Black men for that matter) was taught that there was no time for tears or processing pain which you endured. "Suck it up and keep it moving," was some sort of badge of honor or unwritten mantra. And my life would prove to be the very epitome of sucking it up and keeping it moving because although the emotional scars were there and present in the aftermath of abandonment, secrecy, and pain, it didn't take me out completely, it didn't kill me. But making me stronger was really a lie. It didn't make me stronger, it just made me good at hiding how fragile and damaged I really was.

Bringing my mother to live with my husband, Arthur, (whom I will hereafter affectionately refer to as "The Dude") and me in the summer of 2019 was just the catalyst I needed to push me to face my past head on with no chaser! I had been asking her to move down to Birmingham, AL with us from Philadelphia, PA for at least two years or so because of her myriad health problems, including her increasing battle with COPD, which renders her struggling to breathe from even the smallest exertion of energy. I am my mother's only child and we weren't what one would call close, nevertheless, I didn't want her to suffer with her sicknesses alone. I felt that she wasn't getting a lot of support from family members residing in the area and we had plenty of space for her to be comfortable and not feel isolated. The Dude was very understanding in my need to be able to "put my eyes on her" more closely so we made plans to pack up her belongings and drive the fourteen hours back to Birmingham when she finally agreed to come.

Eventually her presence would prove to be triggering and haunting as I came face to face with all the many issues I had suppressed, repressed, ignored, overlooked, and hidden throughout my life. In time, it would come to my attention, to my chagrin (through therapy and lots of self-reflection), that the pain from these issues were always around, and even in my most veiled attempt to cover them up, they showed themselves strong in many areas of my life. I wasn't fooling anyone but myself. I thought I had overcome most of the very painful moments in my life, including my mom's drug addiction and the scars of mother hurt, attempted sexual abuse by relatives, and wounds of father abandonment. These moments were, in fact, just parading themselves throughout my life with sirens, welcome banners, and yellow caution tape to anyone who was discerning enough to notice. They were probably most evident to those within my own household as they were the beneficiaries of all my pain, in one way or another. I wore this pain on my sleeves, I included it in my relationships, I took it on my jobs, and sometimes it even peeped its head up on my pew at church. And now my pain is ready to testify through the pages of this book.

    How do I even begin to write a book about my life? I've always known that I needed to. Not that I think that my life is any better than anyone else's or that I have achieved so many extraordinary milestones and accomplishments that it warranted being written for mass consumption. But it's the lessons that I have learned, the pain that I have carried and endured, and the grace that I have received that have confirmed for me my need to write it down, to make it plain so that it might help at least one person, then it wouldn't feel like it was all in vain.

Think of this book as your personal invitation to my most important therapy session as I'm sure that this book will be cleansing for my soul. I have dreaded writing it to some degree, procrastinating off and on for at least three years! So, I will hold back nothing, and I am not seeking to spare the feelings of others. Lord knows that I have done that my entire life, leaving me powerless and voiceless as a result. While I do not seek to destroy anyone's reputations, I will tell my story because it's just that - it's MY STORY. I deserve to walk into my own truth and share my bout with brokenness in the hopes that I will finally get free from its bondage and help someone else in the process.

Straight Outta Brokenness, and it didn't kill me! What exactly is brokenness? The Cambridge Dictionary defines brokenness as a condition in which something is badly damaged and unable to continue or work correctly. I am here to defy that definition! The Bible says, "The Lord is close to the brokenhearted and saves those who are crushed in spirit (Psa. 34:18)." This is the story of how, despite the odds stacked against me from the very beginning, the Lord not only showed me how His hand has been upon me before, during, and after every infraction, but He didn't allow the crushing of my spirit to destroy me. I am more than a conqueror. I am healing and I am learning to use my voice so that He continues to get the glory out of my life.

  I invite you to walk with me through this journey of my life. Naturally, as I still live and breathe, the chapters are not all written. There are still daily lessons and struggles that I wrestle with. Hopefully you will be able to take something from my journey that will allow you to see your own as a reflection of God's unmerited favor despite your own obstacles and challenges in this thing we call life.

I. BROKEN PIECES

CHAPTER ONE: Finding Terry

"You may not control all the events that happen to you, but you can decide not to be reduced by them."
-Maya Angelou

Most people probably start the biography of their lives at the beginning; when and where they were born, to whom, etc., but I choose to start a little differently and will revisit the specifics of my genesis a little later. You see, June 29, 2021 was the date everything in my life literally changed in an instant. I was fifty-four years old; five months shy of turning 55, and I unexpectedly came across information that would change the trajectory of the rest of my life. Sounds dramatic, doesn't it? Well, it is. Let me tell you about it.

The previous evening of June 28th I was sitting on my couch doing a little research on my laptop. It was a Monday evening and The Dude (my nickname for my husband, Arthur) was sitting close to me watching television, most likely sports or news. Off and on, since 2010, I had been researching the history of my mother's parents on ancestry. com. I had managed to find out quite a bit about these families, even uncovering a few unknown family secrets and sharing them with family members. It was exciting to see actual historical documents, such as the census reports with my grandparents listed as children with their parents, or my grandfather's Army draft papers with his signature on them. I even uncovered a shocking revelation through a death certificate that my grandmother and grandfather (who were divorced way before I was born) had lost a baby a day after it was born, a year before my mother was born. I don't think any of us knew that!! I had gotten good at finding information and linking them to my family tree. It was like uncovering buried treasure and I enjoyed the hunt. I was also trying to find anything I could dig up on my father, Anthony Mitchell, and his family, since he didn't know his father and couldn't provide any information outside of his name.

This now infamous Monday evening, I had picked up the helm again, determined to see what juicy information

I would discover about past ancestors when suddenly I got an idea that would possibly help me in my search for Anthony's family. If you have taken and submitted your DNA sample to ancestry.com, one of the features of the platform allows you to see matches of others who are related to you genetically. As a shared match, you are also able to view any public family trees they have created. It just so happens that I have thousands of shared DNA matches from closely related to distant relatives.

In 2019 I noticed that a Brian Mitchell appeared at the very top of my DNA matches as a possible first or second cousin (among other possibilities). I reached out to Brian twice in 2019 and once in 2020 via ancestry's inbox to inquire if together we could figure out how we were related and received no response. I figured that since he was a Mitchell, he would be related to Anthony and could somehow provide clues that would lead to Anthony's father. Something in my spirit suggested that I take a different approach this time, since Brian never responded to former requests for collaboration. What if I tried to find out how Brian and I were related on my own by filtering the DNA matches we both shared to see what information we would have in common? I proceeded to do just that. I filtered those matches, and common relatives began to emerge. I noticed a reoccurring name, Florence Palmer, that seemed to be linked to several public trees of our matches. I didn't recognize the name, of course, but things got interesting when I noticed that Florence's niece, Evangeline Palmer, married a John Henry Mitchell, so that gave me hope that this link would lead me to how Brian Mitchell (my strongest DNA match) and my father, Anthony Mitchell, were related. I was sure of it, so I kept digging! The only problem was I didn't know what I was looking for! I knew that Anthony's father's name was James, but his name wasn't showing up on any of the trees I viewed. However, as I continued to dig into the public trees that showed Evangeline and John as spouses, I found something even more incredulous! Have you ever found something and didn't even realize that you were looking for it? Yep. I found something that I didn't even know I was looking for! Let me explain:

    Evangeline and her husband, John Henry Mitchell, were consistently on a few public trees, along with their children. Now, ancestry.com doesn't expose names of any relatives who are still living on members' trees for privacy reasons. However, if a person is listed as deceased, you will be able to see their entire name on a member's public ancestral tree. Only one of Evangeline and John's children was listed by name. On one member's tree, their son Tyrone Mitchell was listed, giving a birth year and date of death. Brian Mitchell's tree (which was being managed by Atiya Mitchell) didn't have any children listed by name. However, Evangeline and John's son (with the same birth and date of death), was listed as Terry Mitchell instead of Tyrone. When I saw the name Terry Mitchell, I suddenly got flushed, my heart began to race, and I couldn't believe what I had read! Wait!!! I stared at the screen for a minute, one long dubious minute. I then got up from the couch with such quickness that The Dude looked at me and said, "What's the matter?" I replied, "I…..I…. I can't believe what I just read. Hold on. I gotta go to the bathroom!" When I returned, I looked at him and I said, "I can't believe what I think I just discovered!"

By now, I'm sure you are like, "Come on, Candie!" Tell us! Whaaaaat is it?" Well, before I get into it, and I promise I will, let me tell you a little story and I think you'll figure it out before I confirm it.

When I was about twelve years old, my mother and I were living with my stepfather, Gary Townsell, Sr., known around North Philadelphia by the moniker, Block. Block and my mother married in my grandmother's living room when I was around four or five years old. The three of us lived first in an apartment on Broad and Erie in North Philadelphia, once with my uncle and his wife and kids on Milne Street in the Germantown area of Philadelphia, and finally landed in a house owned by Block's mother on 12th and Cumberland in North Philadelphia, 1213 Cumberland Street, at which we lived for approximately three or four years. It was easy to remember those three moves because I literally went to a different school for each move. I remember feeling some sense of inward gratification when we moved into 1213 (for some reason in my family we tend to refer to our homes by its house numbers as if it is some sort of nickname). It was a modest sized three-bedroom house, and I had my own room with my own things! At such a young age, I couldn't fully understand why it mattered, but being around friends and family who lived in houses, and comparing that to living in an apartment or staying at a relative's place, I instinctively felt that having our own house was important—and in my mind, it was better!

One evening at 1213, the doorbell rang, and my mom answered the door. Block wasn't home at the time, but a caramel-colored man was standing on the doorstep. He didn't come into the home that I can recall, but I remember my mother saying to me, very matter-of-factly, "This is your father, Anthony Mitchell," as we joined him outside and proceeded to get into his car.

Now let's take a little deep dive into this. I am twelve years old and my mother, up to this point, had NEVER given me any information about my father, no name, no explanations of whereabouts, no excuses for his absence - NOTHING! As a matter of fact, no one in my family ever mentioned a word to me about my father or his identity. I heard no rumors, overheard no conversations, or any allusions to who he was or why I didn't have a father like other kids did. I had already known that Block wasn't my biological father, I was present at their wedding. Sometimes Block and I would have our little silly time together play fighting and what not and I would emphatically announce, "You ain't my father!" as if I had someone else to compare him with. Just imagine being twelve years old and never even knowing your father's name. Now, here we are, and this random man shows up on the doorsteps and my mother announces him as if we had been discussing him all of my life. Just let that settle in your spirit for a minute. I had to stop writing for a minute just to reflect on that myself.

As a child grows, she begins to find a sense of self and/or identity through the relationships around her and through her own personality. Self-esteem building, a sense of belonging, and her local environment, all help to create a sense of self-awareness that she will often take with her throughout her lifetime. Imagine if that child is never given critical information that helps explain who she is or where she comes from and it becomes solely up to her to try to make those connections during the most important times of her development. It is one thing if a parent is deceased. Often in that scenario, the remaining parent will let the child know who her parent was, what happened to him or her, and perhaps even share characteristics about the parent that will help her get a sense of her parent's essence. Even though that child will always have a sense of loss or perhaps feel cheated because she didn't experience the presence of that parent, I can imagine that knowing something about him or her can bring some sense of self-awareness as she tries to marry her own characteristics with those of her absent parent from what she had been told.

But I was told NOTHING! The strange thing to me, other than the fact that I can't believe I was never told anything, was that I never recall even asking! How is that possible? How does a child, especially during those precious inquisitive years, not ask the question, "Where is my daddy?" If I asked, I don't recall asking, and I'm sure I never received an answer that was sufficient for me to remember and take with me through time.

So here we are, my mother, this strange man she called my father, and me. We get into his car, and we drive, not really going anywhere in particular. I just recall sitting in the back of the car as we drove around. Even now I can literally see myself in the back seat while the two of them talked. There was no conversation directed toward me. Also, strange! I did just say that this was my first time hearing about him and meeting him, yet he said nothing to me. What was my twelve-year-old self thinking about this? How was I even processing this? Sir, where have you been? Why haven't you been around? Do you know that I love to read? I was reading the newspaper at five years old, and I didn't even go to kindergarten! Did you know that? My grandmother would boast to her friends and have me read for them and it made me feel super smart! I like to write, too! And I love poetry! My grandmother gave me my first book of poetry by Helen Steiner Rice when I was eight. Do you know my grandmother? When I grow up, I'm going to have two twin girls named A'shaikya and A'shainda. I made those names up because I like making up names for some reason. In the meantime, that's what I call my dolls. Did you know that? Why didn't you come to my surprise twelfth birthday party? It was my very first and only party ever given to me by my family. All my friends from church were here at my house! And I finally got my own record player! I have been wanting one forever! When are you coming back?

   I said none of those things. I said nothing at all. I wasn't asked anything, and I said nothing. After we drove around for what seemed like a very short time, we arrived back at

1213 and my mother and I went into the house. Now here is where my memory gets a little fuzzy: I can't recall if he personally handed me his business card or if I peered at it in my mother's hand, but nonetheless, it simply said, Anthony James Mitchell, Private Investigator, with a phone number. And that, my friends, was the end of that! There was never any other mention of him after that nor did I see him again during my childhood.

Now, I know by now dear reader, because I sense that you are an astute reader, you are saying to yourself, "Self, I still don't understand how this ties into this revelation Candie received on June 28, 2021." You won't get it, yet, but you will soon.

Sometime during that year or the previous year, my memory is fading, my mother conceived twins and miscarried early on in her pregnancy. I remember having to go to my grandmother's while she was in the hospital. While most miscarriages don't result in hospital stays, for some reason hers did. I didn't know the particulars, as I was too young to be told, but I do know she had to have a blood transfusion (an action that later caused her some health issues). I was disappointed at not being able to finally have siblings! I would have made a great big sister! I believe that my mother and Block were having problems in their relationship, not necessarily related to the miscarriage, but something was going on. I know you are still waiting to put your Nancy Drew hat on (I hope you're not too young for that reference) and solve the mystery of my life, but I feel like Block deserves a deeper dive and this might be the perfect intersection to park on. Please forgive me.

Block was quite an interesting character. My mother says she met him while working at a dry cleaner on Columbia Avenue in North Philadelphia, not far from her grandmother's house on Bouvier Street where she grew up. I was just a toddler, and she had her own apartment on Broad and Erie. She moved him in with us, and a few years later, they married in my grandmother's living room.

It wasn't until recently that I discovered the circumstances under which they got together. While I don't know all the details, my mother did share that she helped Block kick his drug habit—heroin, to be specific. Considering nearly 750,000 people were addicted to heroin in the early to mid-1970s, I can't imagine how she managed that, other than being an extraordinary source of support and acceptance. What I do know is that, outside the occasional weed smoking (there were weed plants in the house), I had never seen him do hard drugs nor was he ever, in my presence, under the influence of alcohol.

I credit Block for my writing skills. While my grandmother, Bessie, gets credit for introducing me to poetry and written plays, Block gets honorable mention for my writing journey, at least in the beginning. He was extremely intelligent. Although he claimed to be a Muslim with The Nation of Islam, I watched him read the Bible several times all the way through! He was what I called a fake Muslim! He didn't really practice anything; I think he just liked some of the principles they stood for. I did like it when he sometimes brought home a bean pie or two and it was not uncommon to see the Nation's newspaper, Muhammad Speaks, in our home, but not enough for me to think he was a serious follower. I went to church every Sunday, and he didn't frown upon me going, but I did get the sense that he thought church was a waste of time. He often spoke of the hypocrisy of church goers, especially when it came to my grandmother. I never knew the intricacies of his dislike for her, but I knew he didn't like her and he didn't hide that fact from me or my mother.

I don't know Block's level of education, I assumed he at least graduated from high school, but he checked my homework every night. For English class we had to write definitions and sentences for our weekly vocabulary words. If Block felt that my sentences were "baby sentences," as he called them, he would make me rewrite the sentence until it showed I fully mastered the understanding of the definition. I was livid at having to erase my sentences. I eventually caught on and made sure my sentences were profound, at least profound enough for a pre-teen. He also didn't play about my report card. When report cards came out, I was not allowed to bring home anything but A's and B's. If I brought home a C, I was put on 'punishment' until the next report card came out; a whopping two months later! That's a lifetime for any young person!

What did 'punishment' consist of? I was not allowed to watch television or play outside. When he came home, I was to be found either reading a book or playing in my room. It was awful! Not necessarily the reading or playing in my room, because as an only child, I enjoyed both and could entertain myself for hours! However, not being able to watch television or go outside to play with my friends was just mean, in my opinion! If there was anything I really wanted to watch, my mother would feel sorry for me and let me watch it. She would tell me to hurry to my room if she heard him coming through the door. Punishment life wasn't for me and I quickly learned to stick with A's and B's. I was also a very obedient child and made sure to do as I was told. Block's antics, as they were, led me to love words and loving words (and reading) led to a future of creative writing.

Block did not have a 9-to-5 job. He didn't clock in and out at a business or organization that I knew of. But he did clock in and out every day on the streets. He left early in the morning and he came home every night. He was what was called a "hustler." Now, I couldn't exactly tell you what that meant and what he did, but all I could deduce was that I didn't go without the things I needed and outside of the one-time both my parents were arrested, there was never anything illegal in our home (aside from maybe the marijuana plants, lol). The cops never came to our house and that's all I know about that (inserts laughing emoji).

Okay, I know I just dropped a bomb when I mentioned that both my parents were arrested. Let me take a minute to fill you in. When I was in the second grade, Block, my mother, and I lived on Milne Street in the Germantown section of Philadelphia. I feel as if there was some point at which we lived in that house alone and then were eventually joined by my Uncle Tony, his wife, Ruthie, and their four kids (two of which she had from a previous relationship and two they had together). At any rate, at this time, we were all there together. I honestly can't remember if both of my cousins were born at this time, but I believe at least one of them was.

I couldn't tell you what was going on in that house, because I was not privy to the details, however, I do remember the day it all went south! The cops raided the house and all the adults in the house were arrested. I don't remember if my cousins were there, but I was there and I was taken to the police station separately. Block's mother came to the station to retrieve me (it was interesting to me that my grandmother, Bessie, was not called), and after that incident we moved to the house Block's mother owned at 1213 Cumberland Street. I can't recall if it was immediately after or not, but I do know that I didn't spend my third-grade year in that house.

  I don't think any charges against my mother or Block materialized because we were all back together within a few days and neither of them did any jail time during our years together. Your guess is as good as mine as to what went down, but it was a rather traumatic event for my young mind and one in which, again, I was never given any context, assurances, or asked how it affected me. I suppose I was just expected to be resilient and move on.

  When I was younger, I recall my mother working at the dry cleaner in North Philadelphia for a few years, but from 1972 to 1979 (while married to Block), she did not work. Even though she didn't have a formal job, she did use her hands to be productive for many years. She was a talented seamstress, just like her mother and Aunt Irene. While she often helped them with factory work, she also had her own customers. She was so skilled that she could make men's suits without a pattern! Our house was always filled with fabric, buttons, bobbins, thread, and Butterick and McCall patterns.

I didn't have clothes from the local department store, my mother made many of my clothes, but you couldn't tell. She was so talented that my fifth grade teacher, Ms. Wolfe, would come to my house to get her clothes made. Of course, I was an angel in her class since she had such personal access to my mother! So, between Block's possibly-but-not-proven nefarious day job, my mother's seamstress abilities, and the monthly welfare stipend and food stamps from the government, I was always fully clothed and well-fed. Even though that strange "this-is-your-father" thing happened, I felt somewhat secure living in a two-parent home, in an actual house…. until I didn't.

Sometime after the miscarriage things between my mother and Block must have disintegrated. I do not recall there being a specific incident that caused us to leave. Now, before you think that our time with Block was wonderful and filled with rainbow colored Skittles, let me make something perfectly clear: it wasn't. There were problems and Block was sometimes abusive. Not just the verbal kind, there was also physical abuse.

There were times when he hit my mother but I can confirm that it wasn't a continual occurrence. I can only recall him beating me one time when I lied about eating a cinnamon roll my mother had made. I got the beating of my life with an extension cord, and I can still see remnants of that scar on my thigh today, though it's fading with time (This singular incident is why I am not a liar today). Outside of that, I didn't get beatings, I was a very compliant and mild-mannered child and being put on punishment would always correct my behavior.

Unfortunately, domestic abuse was not uncommon in the 70's. There was this unwritten rule that normalized it, especially in the Black community, and it was common for relatives not to get involved with whatever was going on between a "man and his old lady!" Whatever was going on between Block and my mother, she apparently couldn't take it any longer and was ready to go. I sense that the seemingly out of the blue "this-is-your-father" incident was somehow tied to her need to get out of her relationship with Block, even though I can't confirm it. Somewhere in my gut I think that she saw reconnecting with Anthony as a way out for her and it didn't have anything to do with me. Recently I did ask her why she left Block, and she told me that he had begun using drugs again and it seemed to be getting worse. She did not want to go through that again.

I remember that it was summer when we left. Just that previous Christmas, I recall having the best Christmas I had ever had - right after having a birthday party the month before!! I got EVERYTHING on my Christmas list and then some! I don't know if someone hit the lottery or Block's "hustling" skills were on point that year, but this only child was in heaven! I got a real microscope, a mini piano and was learning to play Auld Lang Syne and Silent Night, lots of clothes that my mother didn't make (including this cream-colored turtleneck and cream corduroy pants that I absolutely loved -AMAZING! I even got my first pair of high heeled shoes), and tons of games! I LOVED board games, and I got almost every board game I wanted: Clue, The Happy Days board game, the Welcome Back Kotter board game, and others. I loved the times we spent, the three of us, playing those games. I had no idea that before the next Christmas, our little family (as imperfect as it was), would be obliterated.

That summer day while Block wasn't home, my mother instructed me to grab a bunch of clothes and put them in several green garbage bags that she handed to me (can we just acknowledge that there is something about putting your belongings in trash bags that is so unsettling). Soon after, my grandfather, Willie, picked us up with all we could carry and drove us to his mother's house at 1721 Bouvier Street - in North Philly. I don't know if Block ever asked us to come back - I don't know what it was like for him to come home and find us gone - or if he was glad to be on his own, but all my pre-teen mind wanted to know was whether or not I was ever going to get all of those wonderful gifts I got that Christmas, in addition to my enormous book collection and other toys. There were promises made to get them to me, and trust me, I asked many times - but they were just empty promises. I never saw any of those things again. The Dude thinks that's why I have had such a hard time in the past being happy at Christmas, thus penning me 'The Grinch.' Maybe there's something to it. I don't know.

We moved into 1721 with my great grandmother, Eliza Tribble, also known as 'Bobbie.' Bobbie's house was a three-story house. On the first floor was our living space which included a living room, dining room, bathroom and kitchen. On the second level were three bedrooms and a bathroom. Bobbie's room was the front bedroom. My mother and I shared a bed in the second bedroom, and Bobbie rented out the back bedroom. She also rented out the two bedroom and bathroom unit on the third floor. Bobbie was a housekeeper for an affluent White family for years, and she was good with her money. Not only did she use her extra space to rent, but she also had a few other houses in the city as rental properties! I now wish I had had the boldness to ask her about her life!

Bobbie was a rather stern woman whom I can't recall ever seeing smile or laugh much. She was a devout Christian and seemingly very respected at her church, Mt. Olive Holy Temple on Broad and Jefferson Street. I wasn't afraid of Bobbie, but she wasn't the easiest to live with. It always felt like we were walking on eggshells around her. It didn't help that my mother always told me that Bobbie didn't care for girls much, she catered to the menfolk in the family. Aside from being a little intimidating, her ability to build wealth and leave a legacy for my grandfather was fascinating to me!

Most things I have found out about her life, I have discovered on ancestry.com. She was born in 1905 in Newberry County, South Carolina where she met my grandfather's father, John Vance Tribble. They married and had my grandfather and his older sister, Mary, in the early 1920's and by 1930 they can be found in the US Census having migrated to a house in Philadelphia with John's cousin and his wife and kids. It is sad that many Black families do not pass down oral history. I would have loved to know anything Bobbie could have told me about her upbringing and her husband, my great-grandfather, who passed away in 1973. I don't remember him at all, but Bobbie did well for herself as a widow. She lived a long life until the age of 97 and got to witness my marriage to The Dude.

When we moved in with Bobbie, it was the beginning of

my middle school journey. I had completed 3rd through sixth grade at George Clymer Elementary School and got accepted into Conwell Middle Magnet School in the Kensington area of Philly for sixth through eighth grade. Conwell was a criteria-based school. You had to have good grades to get in, so thanks to Block, I was a prime candidate. It was also a fun fact that Block's son, Gary Townsell, Jr., also attended Conwell. It was cool to have a "brother" at my school. Traveling to Conwell was a huge trek that took several buses and a train every day! There was no school bus to pick me up and I wasn't driven to school. I was expected to learn bus and train routes and travel alone to get to school each day, which took at least an hour or more one way.

    Parenthetically, it was not uncommon for me to travel the streets of Philadelphia by myself. I had been walking to school by myself since I was in the second grade at John B. Kelly Elementary School in Germantown (approximately a 20-minute walk). In third grade, I walked from 1213 to Clymer. The trek was only a ten or fifteen minute walk, yet it seemed like a long way for a little girl walking alone. I often wondered why my mother would make me walk to school by myself at such an early age; especially when she didn't work and could have just as easily taken me to school and picked me up to make sure I was safe.

I recall one time there were countless news reports warning children not to get into cars with strangers and I was petrified. One day while walking home, I noticed a white car trying to get kids to get in the car. We had all just been dismissed from school and for the most part we were walking in the same direction, though not really walking together. I saw the kids in front of me running, so I ran, too. The car sped away. Even after this event, I was still expected to walk by myself.

My mother was not active at my school, nor did she ever go to parent-teacher conferences. She always sent a note to school that stated she would not be attending and to release my report cards to me, even though there was no real reason why she couldn't show up. That still baffles me to this day. The Dude says it was a different time, we were Generation X, the generation expected to be more independent, the latchkey children. Perhaps. After I had kids of my own, I could never imagine allowing my girls to walk alone to school as early as second or third grade! It has always been a frightening world, even though things became increasingly more dangerous as years progressed.

It might have been around our last year at Bobbie's that the second strange thing happened. And here, my friend, is where the story of June 28, 2021, gets its context. One day I was outside playing, and a man came by the house to see my mother. I remember he was brown-skinned, tall and thin, had a mustache and was rather good looking. I was fascinated because he drove up on a motorcycle. My mother introduced him as "Terry Mitchell, your father." Ok, astute reader, are you still with me? Did you catch that? My mother introduces this man on the motorcycle to me as my father. Why wasn't I "that" kid who said exactly what is on her mind regardless of any pending consequences? Why was I so doggone polite? I said NOTHING! But I wanted to say, "How are you my father when the Private Investigator guy is my father? Mom, don't you remember you told me that?" Again, I don't remember having a real conversation with him either, but I do remember him taking me around the block on his motorcycle. That was my first time on a motorcycle (and my last), and I was scared to death! Unlike Anthony Mitchell, I saw Terry Mitchell on maybe two other occasions.

  The night of June 28 I stood before The Dude telling him that there was a possibility that my highest DNA match, Brian Mitchell, could be related to Terry Mitchell and not Anthony Mitchell. If this is, indeed, a fact, then TERRY MITCHELL, not Anthony Mitchell is my father! I was astounded by this revelation and not even remotely prepared for what would follow on June 29. But one thing is for certain, I would never be the same again.

WORD GIRLZ

I am born again—spiritually transformed and set apart exclusively for God's purpose through the living and abiding Word of God.

" …you have been born again, not of perishable seed but of imperishable, through the living and abiding word of God."
- I Peter 1:23

On October 2, 1977, I gave my life to Christ, a month before my eleventh birthday. The following year I would be introduced to the possible identity of a birth father. Let's be clear when I gave my life to Christ that Sunday evening after watching a movie called, "The Rapture," I was sincere and ready to receive Him into my heart. The Lord knew that I would be ready to accept Him, and although a pre-teen, He had transformed my life and was about to set me apart exclusively for His use - regardless of what I would encounter in years to come, and despite the earthly father(s) that would eventually abandon me. He remained steadfast, constant, and protective!

It is easy to think that when things happen in our lives God is somewhere not paying attention. But that couldn't be farther from the truth! God meets our struggles and our troubles before we do! And not only is He keeping us by the power of the Holy Spirit and His divine Word, but He is already working out our troubles for our good and His glory!

CHAPTER TWO: Invisible: Hiding in Plain Sight

"There's really no such thing as the 'voiceless'. There are only the deliberately silenced, or the preferably unheard."
-Arundhati Roy

I came into this world at somewhere between twenty nine to thirty-two weeks' gestation on Thursday, November 3, 1966, weighing three pounds thirteen ounces. My mother was 15 years old when she found out she was pregnant with me. It was a long time before she had any prenatal care because everyone kept telling her they were too busy to take her to the doctor. In her seventh month, she says she was just going to a routine doctor's appointment and when she got there, she was told that she was in labor. Naturally she didn't believe them because

I wasn't due until January, but they told her if she hadn't come in, I would have come right out onto the street. She told me she had an epidural and that if she had moved while the needle was administered, she could have been paralyzed. I stayed in the hospital in an incubator for preemies and in the hospital for whatever period it took me to come to full-term size. That's all I had been told about my birth. When I was released, I joined my mother at my grandfather's house where she lived with him, his second wife, and her three kids, and one son they shared together (their youngest son was not yet born). I don't have any nor have I ever seen any baby pictures of myself. I've only actually seen a few toddler photos, most of which I received just a few years ago.

I was told that my mother didn't have a crib for me, so I slept in a drawer, something that, to me, is painfully telling about my life. My birth was not celebrated - there were no pretty pink balloons or baby shower games welcoming my entrance into the world; a lack of celebration that would play out over and over again throughout the years to come in more ways than one. Honestly, I don't have much information about the early days of my life, only the pieces that my mother could remember or care to tell me recently. She had a stroke in her early 40's and says it's hard for her to remember some information.

Unfortunately, the information she has forgotten is critical to my understanding of how I got here and how I fit into this world. What I can tell you is that even when she was more lucid and had clarity of memory, she did not share details about my early days with me. She didn't talk about those things with me. At all. It is interesting and not lost on me, that the things I want to know most, things that have to do with me and my origin, or that relate to my father, are the things that she doesn't remember. I don't want to sound cynical, or maybe a part of me does, but I can't help but think that she doesn't want to tell me or there are some pieces that are so embarrassing that she won't tell me. After all she was 15 when she got pregnant by one of two twenty-two year-old father possibilities. There must be something she doesn't want to tell me. There might even be some level of trauma embedded in her story that I don't know about. At any rate, the not knowing haunts me tremendously.

    My earliest memory was in August 1970 when Walter T. Gordy died. Walter T. Gordy was my grandmother Bessie's second husband. Grandmom had my Uncle Tony and my mother with my grandfather, Willie Tribble. They divorced at some point, she had two more daughters, and then she later married Walter, with whom she had a daughter, my mother's youngest sister. Apparently I was close to Walter though I don't remember any moments I shared with him, or anything about him, really. However, the day he died is forever etched in my memory. I was four (almost five) years old, and I recall standing at the foot of his bed while he was having a stroke. I remember the chaos and the screaming. I remember him being placed in an ambulance, and I remember his funeral. There were a lot of people at that funeral. I remember holding my mother's hand and walking up to the casket and I can still see him lying there. That one incident is the reason why I hate funerals to this day. As many funerals as I have had to attend, especially as a pastor's wife, I only go up to view the body if it's family. You're sort of obligated to view family. It is a sight I cannot get out of my mind, and I would much rather prefer to remember people as they were when I last saw them, than laying in a casket.

    I often think I cannot remember Walter because his death overrides my memories. The only evidence of our special bond is a picture I was given recently with him holding my hand as we walked in the water on the beach (you can find it at the end of this chapter). I wonder if my love for the water is attributed to him. When I look at the picture, I feel serene and at peace, just like I do when I am near water. I can sit on a beach and just watch the water for hours. It's absolutely my favorite place in the world. Perhaps that is a gift he gave me in some way.

I don't know if I called him Pop Pop or Grandpop - I can't recall. But I am told he loved me and for that I am grateful. I haven't always felt loved. You know that warm, enveloping love you feel as you grow up with a village of nurturing, protective, and caring adults? Yeah. I haven't always felt that. Growing up I felt cared for in the sense that I was never hungry or without a place to lay my head, but I often felt like an appendage to a family unit- like I was sitting on the periphery of every familial interaction just observing and not really being a part of anything special. I was conditioned to not ask questions and told often to "stay in a child's place," and to be "seen and not heard." I neither felt seen nor heard. I felt invisible. I felt like I was hiding in plain sight. And that invisibility would prove to be a danger zone on more than one occasion. If you learn nothing else from me, please allow the children in your life to be children: encourage their curiosity, answer their questions honestly - regardless of how many there are, and let your presence be a safe and welcoming space so that if things go wrong, they will naturally seek out your protection and not be afraid to approach you.

    I don't want you to think that my entire childhood was complete trash! It was not. The many moves were a breeding ground for the instability my life would take for many years, however, I still had pockets of joy. The sights and sounds of growing up in the '70s and '80s were, in themselves, LOVE! Especially in the summer months! In almost every predominantly Black neighborhood in Philly there was a universal language of love being displayed. Children ran home from school with the same schedule in mind: get your school clothes off, put on your play clothes, and go outside to play until you were called in for dinner! Girls played double Dutch and jacks, while boys played stickball, basketball (with a makeshift basket attached to a telephone pole), or, shucks, any kind of ball! We looked forward to someone turning the water on from the fire hydrant so we could play in the water and splash one another.

    We rode our bikes up and down the street. Mind you I never had a brand-new bike, and especially not the popular Huffy brand it seemed everyone else had. I had what we called a "bus," handed down by the white family my great-grandmother cleaned houses for. It didn't have a white basket, a bell, or the tassels hanging from the handlebars like I wanted. It was clunky and just not attractive, but I rode it anyway! I was a tomboy for sure and I was prone to ride a skateboard, roller skate, and even climb a tree. We played games like Hot, Cold, Butterbean, and Tag, You're It! There was always someone playing music on the block, but especially on Saturdays.

Saturday mornings were cleaning days for most families. Your mother would get you up early to do your chores (if you weren't already up watching cartoons and eating cereal), and you couldn't go outside until you finished. You would see everyone's mother sweeping in front of their house and washing the steps down with Comet or Ajax while someone blasted their music through the window. The sounds of Motown, the Philly Sound by artists such as The Stylistics, O'Jays, Patti LaBelle, Teddy Pendergrass and more, could be heard throughout the neighborhood. Saturday evenings were special, too. Adults would bring out a card table and play cards, or you could see families sitting on their steps while kids played in the street. I didn't know the word for it then, but I do now: it's called community.

There was a sense of family and community on each block. Neighbors looked out for each other and each other's kids. Sometimes too much! There was always that one old lady on the block who was ready and willing to tell your mother that you were misbehaving on the block! I made sure to keep my nose clean but plenty of kids got a whooping when a neighbor tattled.

My favorite memories were the family reunions. For several years I can remember my grandmother and her siblings having a family reunion in New York with all the nieces, nephews, grandchildren, and cousins. My great aunt, Aunt Dorothy, was my favorite aunt and she lived in a swanky high-rise apartment with a beautiful view on Lenox Avenue in New York City. Her daughter, Claire, and her husband, Eddie, would host the reunions at their house in Long Island, New York. All the Philly relatives would crash at Aunt Dorothy's the night before. All you could see were pallets of blankets and pillows anywhere there was room. We would head out to Long Island the next day by caravan. The weekend was always filled with lots of fun and games. It was wonderful to see my family all together and enjoying each other's company. The only other time we all got together like that was for Thanksgiving, usually hosted by Aunt Irene, my grandmother's sister or her brother, Uncle Archie.

Eventually, my mother stopped going to the reunions and to Thanksgiving get-togethers. I have no idea why, but I suspect it was because there were two sides to our small family. There were the religious folks, which included my grandmother, Aunt Dorothy, Uncle Archie, and Aunt Gladys, and the other side was any of their kids who didn't go to church. I suspect Aunt Irene was also on the non-church-going side because I don't ever remember her going to church regularly. The non-churchgoers wanted to smoke, drink, etc. and since they couldn't do that in the presence of the elders, they eventually stopped attending the reunions. At some point we stopped having large gatherings altogether. I think the last reunion I went to as a child, I was about nine or ten. I do recall my grandmother hosting the family for Thanksgiving as I got older, but by that time I had a family of my own and was living out of town.

My cousin Sherri and I would go to visit my Aunt Dorothy in New York on a few occasions, accompanying her to Broadway plays. I fell in love with the theater because of her.

Aunt Irene would let me stay over her house when I was younger as well. She was funny but I was low key afraid of her sometimes. She was very vocal and said whatever it was that was on her mind, even criticism, but I liked her. She had a live-in boyfriend, whom we called Uncle Raleigh.

One weekend, when I was about eight or nine years old, I went to spend the night at her house. I had gotten up early on Saturday morning to go watch cartoons while Aunt Irene was still asleep. As I was watching TV, Uncle Raleigh came downstairs and asked me to come sit on his lap. I didn't think anything of it, so I complied. I remember I had on a cute light blue pajama set, a satin-like top with matching shorts. I went to sit on his lap with my eyes still fixed on the cartoons. A few minutes went by and he told me to get up. I noticed my shorts were wet, which was obvious because they were so silky. He instructed me to go change and hand him my pajamas so he could put them in the washing machine, but not to wake up my aunt on my way upstairs. I remember distinctively looking into her room and she was still asleep with the patches she would often wear to bed, nestled on her eyes. I didn't know what to think about what had transpired. He didn't touch me (I do remember being shifted around on his knee at some point), so it didn't register to me that this grown man had placed me on his lap to masturbate on my pajamas. My eyes were so fixed on the cartoons that I didn't notice what he was doing. However, even though I didn't have the tools to process what had transpired, I instinctively knew it was something that shouldn't have happened. Traumatic events can be very subtle and even though he didn't molest me, there was still a sexual act involved which stripped a level of my innocence away. And that was the beginning of my awareness that grown men could be inappropriate with young girls.

Therapy has helped me to see how incidents such as the "Uncle Raleigh" interaction set me on a course of being silent whenever things were done to me by family. It wasn't that I wasn't brave enough to tell, because I wasn't scared. But I was always concerned about how my life would end up if I spoke up - not having too many people I could count on to take care of me if my mother went off the deep end for finding out and being put in jail for either causing them harm or getting someone else to cause them harm - that was my biggest and only fear.

Inappropriate touching happened again with two other family members when I was a teenager. Those times, however, I was determined to let them know that I wasn't going to be a victim. "If you don't stop, I'm going to scream!" For both offenders this was enough to ward them off (even though one of them tried more than once but got the message as I got more aggressive with my threats), however, I never told anyone else. The crazy thing is I didn't avoid being in their presence or anything afterward. Don't get me wrong, I was never in their presence by myself, but in my mind I had said what I needed to say and let them know I was taking control of my own body. I simply internalized that this was how men were and though I didn't tell on them, I also felt empowered to stand up for myself if I needed to.

I did just that years later as a young adult when grown, married "church" men said inappropriate things to me to see if I was "that type of girl." Even though I wasn't violated physically, for many years to come I distrusted the intentions of most male suitors, believing they only wanted one thing; most of the time, I was right.

On one occasion a visiting preacher came to our church to do a revival and hung out with me, my aunt, and her boyfriend afterward. I didn't think anything of it when he asked me to accompany him to church the following day. He asked me to come meet him at his hotel room and we would leave from there. I got to his room, and he was on the phone talking to his wife, so naturally I waited patiently. After he got off the phone, he asked me to come sit by him on the bed. I looked at him like he was crazy and said, "No, I'm good. Are you ready to go?" He quickly got the message, gathered his things, and we went to the church. I was furious! Yes, I was undoubtedly naive! Why didn't I consider that it wasn't a good idea to meet this grown, married man in his hotel room? Because I was just naive enough to think that men of God were honorable. I learned that day that not all of them are and I never put myself in that situation again. What irked me even more about this event was the fact that I think that predator tried to insinuate to my aunt and her boyfriend that something happened between us! How dare he? And furthermore, how dare my aunt and her boyfriend believe that I would do such a thing!!! I did confront him, gave him a few choice words, and never spoke to him again!

Even though in my own way, I had stood up to these individuals, these relatives of mine, this preacher, and the married men at my church, it all played into a persistent feeling of not being seen nor heard, which further evoked in me a profound sense of isolation and invisibility. I often wondered what it was about me that would make these people that were supposed to be trustworthy, supposed to protect me from predators, want to violate me? Why was I being singled out? I keep coming back to two things: 1) they were SCUM, and 2) I was the child sitting on the margins, silent and unprotected. I was easy prey. It's as if my presence was overshadowed by a perpetual sense of insignificance.

   As I ponder these things, I feel a cascade of emotions, ranging from frustration and sadness to anger and a tinge of resentment. So many years I have wasted by yearning for validation and longing to be acknowledged, valued, or just asked, "How are you? What's going on with you?" Over time, I have realized how these unmet needs eroded my self-esteem, making me question my self-worth and abilities.

   I didn't grow up with a lot of "I love you's" and positive affirmations. My mother was sometimes low key verbally abusive, and to be honest I don't think she meant it, but she would say I was stupid when I did something wrong, or "slow as molasses" with such disdain when I didn't move as fast as she wanted (which is probably the reason why I'm one of the most punctual people you will ever know), or just abrasive when something wasn't going right in her own life. One of the things that irked me the most was hearing her talk on the phone about me if I had done something. Why wasn't I praised for the good things I did? Why wasn't I encouraged more than scolded? Words hurt, words wound, and words destroy. The biggest lie we were told when we were kids was to recite and believe the saying, "Sticks and stones may break my bones, but names will never hurt me." Well, every time I was called anything but my name, it hurt me!

The Dude could tell you stories about how deep those words, "Are you stupid?" were etched in my spirit. It made me very defensive, and my reply in many conversations, especially with The Dude, would be, "I know! I'm not stupid!" One day The Dude (recognizing that my response was deeper than a simple reply) said, "I KNOW you're not stupid. No one thinks you're stupid. No one else sees you that way!" It took him saying that to me, validating me, really seeing ME, for me to accept it and begin to believe that I was worthy of being seen and that the margins were no place for me. Never again would I let anyone make me feel like it was but it took me a long time to get there.

WORD GIRLZ

I declare that I am seen, known, and valued by the Almighty God. I am validated through Jesus Christ, and His love defines my worth.

"O, Lord, you have searched me and known me! You know when I sit down and when I rise up; you discern my thoughts from afar." God's eyes are ever upon us, and His gaze is one of unwavering love and compassion (Psalm 139:1-2).

In our journey of faith, it is often easy to lose sight of our true worth and significance. We may find ourselves striving for acceptance and validation in the eyes of others, seeking worldly measures of success and significance. However, as believers, we are called to remember that our ultimate value and validation comes from God alone.

Imagine for a moment the vastness of the universe, with billions of stars and galaxies, yet the same God who created it all also knows each of us intimately. God, in His infinite wisdom and knowledge, sees us in a way that no human ever could. He sees beyond our outward appearance, accomplishments, and failures, into the depths of our hearts (Psalm 139:1-2).

As the Creator of all things, God has instilled intrinsic value within each one of us. We are fearfully and wonderfully made (Psalm 139:14). Our worth does not depend on the opinion of others or the standards of this world. In fact, we were created in the very image of God Himself (Genesis 1:27). Our value is not determined by our accomplishments or failures, but by our identity as beloved children of God. We are precious in His sight, and nothing can diminish the infinite worth He has placed upon us.

To fully grasp the significance of God's view of us, we must align our perspective with His. We are called to see ourselves through the lens of God's love and acceptance, to view others with compassion and understanding, and to pursue a life that reflects His character. As we deepen our relationship with Him through prayer, studying His Word, and fellowship with other believers, we will grow in our understanding of how God sees us.

top left, bottom right: Tyrone Machio Palmer Mitchell, top right, bottom left: Candie

This is me with my grandmother's husband, Walter T. Gordy. I was told that we were really close. Unfortunately, I can't recall and only remember watchimg him suffer a stroke in front of me three months before my 5th birthday. I also remember seeing him in the casket at his funeral. Both events had a profound and lasting effect on me. But as I look at this photo so many things come to mind, one being my absolute love of being near water and the peace and security I feel when I am. They say your body holds onto memories, so perhaps this photo explains why.

Toddler Candie. It seems that the toddler stage is the only stage that I have seen pictures of myself. I have never seen newborn or infant photos.

The last family reunion I recall my mom attending. I was about 9 or 10 years old.

CHAPTER THREE: Absent Dad and Mother Wounds

"A child's greatest emotional need is to feel loved and protected by its mother."
- Sigmund Freud

If you grew up with a loving, present, and protective father, then you, my friend, are indeed blessed beyond measure. If you grew up with a father that you didn't quite get along with, but he was a provider and protector, and loved you the best way he knew how, then you are also blessed beyond measure. And if you grew up with both a loving mother and father, then in my opinion, you won the lottery! Growing up without a father, or not knowing your father, is surely a hard experience to endure. Strong familial relationships, characterized by unconditional love, support, and a sense of belonging, play a crucial role in promoting resilience and well-being in children and adolescents. Having a nurturing and supportive family environment helps young people navigate the challenges they face and develop into healthy and resilient individuals.

As a Black female child, the void of not having a father, or many Black male role models in my life, left me open to abuse, promiscuity, and to being taken advantage of. Statistics have shown that fatherless children are at higher risk of having emotional and psychological issues: a father's absence can contribute to feelings of abandonment, rejection, and loss. It is not uncommon for fatherless children to struggle with issues related to self-esteem, identity, and forming healthy relationships. They may also experience higher levels of anxiety, depression and loneliness. Research has shown that they may also have behavioral problems, educational challenges, social and interpersonal difficulties, and are at a risk for living their entire lives in poverty. But for me, God said, "NO!" Society might say that I was destined to be an unwed mother, I was destined to be a product of my environment, of the brokenness in my home, but God said, "NO!" I was not promiscuous, I chose my friends wisely, and I was what one would call a "church girl." Even in that, I didn't come out unscathed by my father's absence nor my mother's (or family's) inability to nurture and prepare me for the world.

Now, let's be clear: I am not writing this book to blast my parents or my family for what they did or did not do, rather I want to show you that regardless of how the odds seem stacked against you, no matter what trials and tribulations you've experienced, there is still hope - and when God says, NO, he means NO! I have some scars; yes, I have had some issues with abandonment, having been abandoned by my mother at a point, and by not one but two potential daddies (several times at that)! But God has been good to me! He kept me even when I didn't want to be kept! He provided for me when no one else could or would. He gave me favor and has always showered me with His steadfast love even in my most dire circumstances.

After a few short years, my mother and I left my great grandmother's house to go live in West Philadelphia with my grandfather and at one point there were about 11 people in that 3-bedroom house, including us. My grandfather's house on Chestnut Street in West Philadelphia was always open to family members who were in transition. I don't know how we did it, but we did. At one point my mother and I slept on a bed that was put in the dining room downstairs between the living room and kitchen. Can you say, "NO PRIVACY?!" I sure can. Then I recall having to sleep on the couch when my mother left me (we will get into those details shortly), sharing a room with my cousins - three to one bed, and finally having a room to myself when my aunt and her kids and two of my uncles moved out. What a mess for a young teenaged girl who started off living with two parents and having her own room to sharing a bedroom with her mother, and then moving into a house with what seemed like a million other people.

No one explained how this transition might be for me nor explored the shock to my world the breakup of my mother and stepfather would be. No one talked to me about it at all. No one seemed to care that there was an actual effect on me. Kids are often just expected to adapt and be resilient without explanation or provided context to help them navigate change in their lives and routines. Therefore, it was no different for me.

The numbered streets in Philadelphia run north south and are typically organized in numerical order from east to west as you move away from the Delaware River, which is on the eastern side of the city.

The named streets typically run east west and are given names instead of numbers. These named streets are often named after trees, famous individuals, or landmarks. Market Street is a central east-west street that divides the city into north and south. Streets to the north of Market Street are designated as "North," for example North 5th

Street, while streets to the south are designated as "South," as in South 5th Street. My grandfather's house was on Chestnut Street, in the 59 hundred block between 59th Street and 60th Street in West Philadelphia. "West Philly" is probably most known to outsiders because of Will Smith's reference to the area in The Fresh Prince of Bel Aire's opening theme song. Having lived in North Philly, and in the Germantown section of the city, West Philly was architecturally different. The streets were much wider, making way for at least two (and in some instances, three) lanes of traffic for cars and buses, while North Philadelphia streets were much more narrow and the houses seemed much closer together.

The streets in West Philadelphia seemed so wide that I can honestly say I didn't know anyone on the other side of Chestnut Street. I knew all the families that made up our side of the street and most around the corner. It's as if our lives only consisted of one side of the street. I had known many of the families most of my life. There were a lot of kids and teens in this one block radius, and we all interacted in one way or another. Back in those days people came outside and sat on their steps while children played.

The Harris family lived closer to the corner of 59th Street. I can't quite pinpoint when the Harrises moved onto Chestnut Street, but they weren't around during my younger years. Mr. and Mrs. Harris had a rather large family, if I remember correctly, with six or maybe seven children. However, I only really got to know the four who were still living at home: Stephanie, her twin brother affectionately known as Pip, Nelda, and Angela, whom we fondly called "Angie." Angie was the same age as I was and we quickly became inseparable. She was a bundle of energy and not afraid to speak her mind. She was always great company, and I admired her kind heart. Angie had a fair complexion sprinkled with freckles, just like many in her family, and I thought it was the most endearing thing!

 I can't quite recall why our friendship eventually drifted apart, but when it did, that's when Stephanie (who was older) and I grew closer. We became best friends, and she even started coming to church with me, much to her mother's dismay since they were raised Catholic and my church, Faith Tabernacle Holiness Church, was a Pentecostal church located at 19th & Susquehanna Avenue in North Philadelphia. Mrs. Harris didn't stop her from going with me and I was extremely grateful for that because Stephanie came to know Christ through our church's ministry.

 Also nestled in our neighborhood were the Blands. The Bland family seemed like the anchor to the entire neighborhood. The Blands consisted of Mr. and Mrs. Bland

and their six children. Mrs. Bland was Native American and Mr. Bland was Black. Their children were a wonderful mix of the two, some looking more like their mom, and some like their dad. I can't recall a time when I didn't know the Blands. The majority of the Bland children were much older than I but I knew Bobby, Sharon and Lisa the best. Sharon Bland was like the neighborhood auntie. Sharon looked just like her mother and wore her jet-black silky hair in one ponytail all the way down her back to her tailbone with a bang in the front. Never having married or had children of her own, Sharon watched out for all of us in the neighborhood. She was a beautiful soul and I'm glad I got a picture with her a few years before she passed.

Bobby Bland was my uncle, Quinzell's, best friend so I saw him a lot growing up and remember when he passed away. Lisa Bland was the closest to my age (I would later find out that her husband and The Dude are cousins.) Even when I didn't live in West Philadelphia, I loved coming back to chat with Lisa or Sharon. It was very nostalgic to do so.

The one person that I watched and admired while living at my grandfather's house was my Aunt Sheila. Sheila, Jerome, and Steve were not my grandfather's biological children, yet he raised them and he's always been "dad" to them. Quinzell and Boniticio were my grandfather's kids with his wife, Lucille. There was just something about Sheila: she was beautiful, she was intelligent, she had a good job at a doctor's office, and despite raising her two children (at the time) by herself, she had that "it girl" aura. I just really liked her and her bubbly personality, and she was always kind to me. Both of her kids, Carlethia (whom we called Lucy), and Tyrone (whom we called Buster) were younger than I and went to Catholic school. I think that watching her helped me understand that I could do anything I put my mind to. Sheila would go on to have two more children, Juanita (who was with me all the time when she was a toddler) and Coleman, and though she would eventually battle some pretty strong demons in her life, her former self would remain an inspiration for me.

At one point while we were living at my grandfather's, my mother left me. She had been seeing this guy named Larry and she left to move in with him. They first had an apartment over the top of a cleaners in another part of West Philadelphia. I went a few times to visit but was totally unimpressed. Then he moved her into a house in an area of West Philadelphia called, "The Bottom." It became known as "The Bottom" because it was the bottom part of West Philadelphia. The area, during this time, didn't have a great reputation and was considered a blight in West Philadelphia. Today, because of gentrification, it is now called Mantua, Powelton Village, and University City. I had only heard negative stories about the area, so I didn't want to live there! When I went to "visit" the house where my mother and Larry were, there was no gas on, which meant there was also no hot water. I was definitely not impressed with having to heat water or food on a hot plate in order to wash and make food. Honestly, I don't recall how the conversation even went when she left me at my grandfather's, if there was a conversation. I did not like Larry and I felt a sense of abandonment by my mother, believing that she chose him over me. My mother and I didn't have an adorable mother/daughter relationship like you see on social media in our current day. She was not a nurturer, she didn't provide hugs and kisses, or words of affirmation. She wasn't basking in my latest accomplishments (at least not to me) and I didn't feel special. I often felt like I had to maneuver around her emotions and whatever it was that she was going through at the time. I'm sure she was only using the tools she had at her disposal. Mother wounds are often generational, and it was a passed down trait to her.

Rhona Lewis, in her article about mother wounds, writes, "Children (usually daughters, but sometimes also sons), are said to experience a mother wound if their mother:

- provided support by taking care of the physical needs

of the children, but didn't give love, care, and security
- didn't provide empathy to mirror the child's emotions and help them label and manage those emotions
- didn't allow the child to express negative emotions
- was extra critical
- expected the child's support with their own physical or emotional needs
- wasn't available to the child either because they had to work or because they were busy with their own interests (You can, however, be a working mom - even a working single mom - without instilling the mother wound!)
- had suffered emotional or physical abuse themselves, didn't process the trauma, and was, therefore, unable to nurture and offer love
- had an untreated mental health condition
- experienced alcoholism or drug addiction."[1]

Throughout various stages of my life, my mother embodied at least five of these qualities. The one that resonates with me the most is the first one: my mother provided support by taking care of my physical needs, but she didn't give love, care, and security. One of the things that annoyed me the most was the fact that she had no

---

1   Lewis, Rhona. "The Mother Wound: What It Is and How to Heal." Healthline, 29 Sept. 2020, https://www.healthline.com/health/mother-wound#who-has-it

problem sending me to do things that were not in my best interest or putting me in situations that could have had dire consequences on my life. One such instance (though there were others), was while living at my grandfather's (I was about 14), she would send me to the corner store to cop weed for her.

The corner store was owned by a Jamaican guy whom everyone knew sold drugs out of the store as well. She would send me to the store for her cigarettes and a "nickel or dime bag" of weed. I instinctively knew this was wrong on so many levels and felt so uncomfortable doing it for her. One of the things that was clear in the streets was that the weed house or the place that sold weed was a target - for cops and robbers! Aside from the fact that it was immoral for her to send me, it was also illegal and dangerous! What if something happened while I was there? Suppose it was the exact time that someone wanted to rob him? I'm pretty sure the owner was armed as well, and bullets have no names on them! After a while I got up the courage to just tell her, 'No! I didn't want to do it anymore.' She looked at me a little crazy, but she knew it wasn't right, that I was right, and she stopped making me go.

Her own upbringing was unstable as she wasn't raised by her mother. According to the family legend, relayed to me by both my grandfather and mother, my grandparents went through a divorce, and during a custody hearing, my mother and uncle were awarded to my grandfather. While my Uncle Tony was already with him, my mother was supposed to be placed in his custody at an agreed-upon time. However, instead of honoring this arrangement, my grandmother took my four-year-old mother to a friend's house and left her there for days. My grandfather, once he found out, retrieved her and brought her to his mother's house, where she was raised once he was awarded primary custody of both children. My mother always wished for a relationship with her mother and briefly stayed with her around the age of thirteen. At that time, my grandmother had remarried and had given birth to my aunt.

During this stay, my mother said she felt like a live-in babysitter and maid, responsible for her little sister and household chores. This arrangement lasted approximately a year or two until one day my grandmother sent her to the store, and somehow my mother got in touch with my grandfather and informed him that she would run away if she were forced to return. My grandfather didn't make her go back and allowed her to move in with him, his wife Lucille, and her children. She initially stayed on the couch in their small apartment until they all moved together to the house on Chestnut Street. There is a lingering hint of resentment in my mother's voice when she recalls this period in her life. It's evident that my mother felt abandoned by her mother, just as I have experienced feelings of abandonment from her. It's worth noting that my grandmother, too, went through abandonment from her own mother, who left her and her four siblings to move to New York City, leaving them in their father's care for a period. While I don't have precise details about my grandmother's age at the time or how long their mother was gone, it's reasonable to assume that, being the youngest, she also felt abandoned by her mother. At least on the surface, it seems that the theme of motherly abandonment has been recurring in our family across generations. However, it's weird to me that this pattern of maternal abandonment only shows itself in my grandmother's relationships with her children and not in her siblings' relationships with their offspring, at least not to my knowledge. I get the sense that my mother felt abandoned by both of her parents. Despite my grandfather's constant presence in her life, he "chose to raise someone else's kids," in her own words. In my opinion, having him present and showing up for her in her times of need at all was a blessing, something I couldn't help but notice was absent and wish for in my own life.

 My mother's life with Larry came to a halt after one big, public argument around the corner from my grandfather's house. I was in the house babysitting my little cousin when another cousin came running into the house to tell me that Larry had hit my mom and had her pinned up against the wall. I was probably around fourteen or fifteen years old and clearly not thinking straight. I ran to the kitchen impulsively and grabbed a knife. With my little cousin positioned on my hip and yielding a knife in the other hand, I dashed out the house, around the corner, and screamed, "You better take your hands off my mother!" By this time there was a whole crowd of neighbors circling the action, so he let her go and walked away. I'm sure he was more concerned about the looming crowd, than the teenage girl holding a knife with a toddler on her hip! I realize now how ridiculous I must have looked to this grown man, but at the time, I felt pretty big and strong! I didn't like him anyway! My mother moved back into my grandfather's house and our lackluster coexistence continued. To say the least, I was ecstatic that the loser was gone. However, I still didn't feel close to my mother. We were surrounded by a host of relatives and my main goal was just staying out of people's way! I felt like my grandfather's wife didn't like me too much, so I was respectful, but chose to keep my distance whenever possible. It didn't help that my mother told me that they had a falling out when I was about two because my mother thought she tainted my milk somehow. I have no idea if that was true or not, but she gave me the sense that she didn't care for me or my mother.

My mother was in the process of rebuilding her life, and Aunt Sheila helped her secure a job at a doctor's office on 60th Street. While my aunt worked for the medical doctor, my mom worked for the podiatrist. I was thrilled when she eventually announced that we were moving into our own apartment. It was a two-bedroom unit located on 60th and Locust Street, just above a Jamaican store that sold oils and incense. This new place was only a few blocks away from my grandfather's house. The best part was that I had my own room again! I was so excited that my mom allowed me to decorate it myself, that I filled the walls with photos of my friends, cutouts of my favorite celebrities from the latest Right On! magazines, and my cherished album covers. It was truly MY ROOM!

The only downside was that you had to pass through my room to access my mother's, so it wasn't entirely private, but it still felt like my sanctuary. In that apartment, I felt like my mother and I were finally going to grow closer. It was there that she made a declaration I would never forget, saying, "It's me and you against the world!" Those words meant the world to me as a teenager yearning for more connection with the adults in my life, especially my mother. It signified that she wanted me by her side, that we were in this journey of life together, just the two of us. We didn't have a lot of money, so there were no trips, vacations, or outings. Instead, my mother went to work, and I went to school (or church), and we returned home together.

Our apartment was modest but always clean. In addition to the two bedrooms, it had a bathroom, a spacious living room, and a full-sized kitchen. I may not have had the latest or greatest things, but my basic needs were always met. I couldn't afford extras like a school jacket, but I had the essentials. While we did enjoy the occasional indulgence in fast food, most of our meals were prepared at home. My mother was particularly skilled in the kitchen, which makes it somewhat perplexing that she never taught me how to cook. Surprisingly, my family was full of talented cooks, yet none of them ever took the initiative to teach me this valuable life skill or engage in cooking activities with me as a child or teenager. Consequently, once I ventured out on my own, I turned to cookbooks as my culinary guides. Fortunately, I had a knack for following recipes diligently, so my lack of culinary training rarely showed. However, despite the strong connection I was hoping to forge with my mother, our relationship eventually took a different turn, and that deep bond I wanted never fully materialized.

The first big change was when my mom opened our home to my uncle's girlfriend, Eloise, and her two young sons. I liked Eloise. She was bubbly, very fashionable, and could

SANG! I loved to sing so listening to her croon was fun for me! Eloise's older son had some mental delays, but he was a sweet boy. Her youngest son, Mark, was my uncle's son and he was a baby when they moved in with us. Eloise and her sons slept in a pullout couch in the living room. I liked Eloise though it seemed that drama followed her, specifically through her relationship with my uncle. They argued a lot and there was always some tension between the two of them, specifics of which I was too young to know about. I also became the in-house babysitter. By this time, I was everybody's babysitter, and I was good at it. During the summer, I was watching five kids - Eloise's two sons, my cousin, Nita (Aunt Sheila's daughter), and my other aunt's two sons. This is how I made my pocket change.

  My mom and Eloise started going out to the cabaret on Thursday nights (ladies' night) every week. I would watch the boys and make sure they ate and were put to sleep. I noticed my mom started partying more and more and our relationship was pretty much nonexistent by this time. I spent most of my time in my room, at school, church, or with my church friends. She would let me spend the night over church member's houses, but outside of that I wasn't allowed to do much more. I had to come straight home after school and wasn't given permission to do extra-curricular activities.

My biggest regret was not being able to participate in any after-school functions. I attended THE Philadelphia High School for the Creative and Performing Arts, often referred to as CAPA. It was a new school dedicated to the arts, offering majors in drama, dance, creative writing, vocal, instrumental music, and visual art. The school was established in 1978 under the leadership of our first principal, John R. Vannoni. I joined as a freshman in 1980 and am a member of a group known as "The Originals," consisting of students who were part of the first graduating classes from 1980 to 1985. Our school was originally located in the Atlantic Building at Broad and Spruce Streets, where we shared space with the Philadelphia College of the Arts. In 1980, during my freshman year, the movie "Fame" was released, followed by a TV series in 1982. Whenever people asked me which school I attended and I replied CAPA, they often wondered if it was like "Fame." Without hesitation, I enthusiastically responded with a resounding "YES!"

CAPA held a special place in my heart; it was an incredible gift during the most challenging period of my life. It brought together a diverse group of talented, independent, and unique individuals who were passionate about honing their skills and fostering creativity in a non-judgmental, safe, and nurturing environment. At CAPA, it was a common sight to see dancers practicing in the hallways or spontaneous song sessions erupting in the lunchroom. The atmosphere was brimming with youthful dreams and boundless creativity. Since the school was relatively new, there weren't options for double majors or major-minor combinations. Consequently, despite having a talent for singing, I was confined to my chosen major, creative writing. Writing held a special place in my heart, a passion that was sparked by my grandmother who gifted me my first book of poetry by Helen Steiner Rice on my 8th birthday. My mother wasn't much of a reader and hadn't finished high school, yet she made sure I had access to plenty of books, fostering my love for reading.

    Creative writing majors at CAPA were exposed to various forms of writing, including poetry and journalism. During high school, I realized my preference for creative writing over journalism, as the latter didn't allow me to fully unleash my creative talents. At CAPA, it was typical for students to gravitate toward others in their own majors. I had a close-knit group of friends in the creative writing program, which included Marie, Jennifer, Kim, and Tanya. Marie, Jennifer, and Kim were in the same grade as I, while Tanya was a year younger. We were typical teenagers who enjoyed reading Harlequin Romances but also relished creating our own stories. One of us would initiate a story in a composition book, crafting a diverse set of characters and scenarios, and then pass it on to the next person to continue the narrative. I absolutely loved participating in these creative ventures; they greatly expanded my imagination and my writing skills.

After school, my friends would go hang out or gather at nearby corner stores in Center City to play video games like Miss Pac-Man and Galactica, which were quite popular at the time. Unfortunately, I couldn't join them because I was instructed to head straight home after school. I longed to be part of the Yearbook Committee or simply hang out with other students, but I never had the chance to engage in any after-school activities. The only time I didn't feel completely left out was when the soap opera "General Hospital" gained popularity with the Luke and Laura storyline. Everyone, and I mean EVERYONE, both girls and boys alike, would rush home to watch the drama unfold, so we could talk about it at school the next day. Now that I am older and looking back, it's astonishing to me that we were rooting for a love story that developed between a rapist and his victim. I'm sure that today, Luke would have definitely been at the top of the list of our current cancel culture. And rightfully so!

When I wasn't in church, at a church member's house, or at school, I was home. During my last year of high school,

I was allowed to have a little more freedom. I got a job to make a little money for myself. I worked from five pm to nine pm on Thursdays and Fridays (and some Saturdays) at a telemarketing company on City Line Avenue. It was important to me not to have to ask my mother or anyone else for money to get the things I needed or wanted. I also got to sing Gospel after school with some of the vocal majors for a group we formed that sang at Heavenly Hall, a gospel night club of sorts. We sang at different places and events throughout the city.

At some point Eloise and her sons moved into an apartment with my uncle and they subsequently broke up. However, my mother met her boyfriend, who happened to be Eloise's cousin, at one of those cabaret parties. His nickname was "Be Cool." It didn't take long to realize why Be Cool, of South Philadelphia, was given the nickname. He thought he was cool! He was, in my opinion, an average looking man with a huge mole on the side of his nose. He loved to laugh and tell jokes. I didn't dislike him at first. He was okay, I suppose. But I liked him less when my mother moved him into our apartment. I didn't understand why he had to move in. He had two kids (boy and girl twins) of his own and they came over a few times, but they were younger than I was. It was Be Cool that introduced my mother to crack cocaine, and from there things just went badly. And that's the second time I felt my mother abandoned me. She chose him and drugs over me.

If there is anything worse than not having a father to protect you, love on you, or just show up for you, it must be having a mother who isn't doing it either. While I won't go through all of the sordid details of how my mother's and Be Cool's drug addiction showed up in our home on a daily basis (let's just say it was a LOT), I will share how it made me feel. I felt alone, I felt pushed aside, and I felt invisible. Their addiction wouldn't allow them to see me - a young teenage girl who needed someone to step in and guide her through her last years in high school and into young adulthood. I ran to church (Sundays, Tuesdays, and Fridays) to get away from the instability and toxicity at home. Everyone knew my mother was battling with drugs: church members, family members, and neighborhood friends. I don't know if it was because she wasn't strung out - she was functional, that people didn't intervene. No one scooped me up to make sure I was okay. No one stepped in. No one championed for me. No one asked me HOW I WAS DOING!!! It was business as usual: church as usual, family as usual, friends as usual. I looked okay on the outside, but I WAS NOT OKAY!

My Pastor, Albert Blassingame, Sr, was probably the only one who tried to look out for me, who offered me empathy.

His concern for my well-being during those crazy years will never be forgotten. He made sure I got home safely many nights after church.

Our church was located at 2204 N. 19th Street right at Susquehanna Avenue and my mother and I lived at 60th and Locust Streets. That's about seven miles. I took the 60th Street El train downtown to the subway line, got off at Susquehanna Avenue and then most times walked from Broad and Susquehanna to 19th Street if the bus wasn't coming, which was most of the time. I did this on Sundays, Tuesdays, and Fridays to attend church services and to get out of the house as much as possible. Sometimes I traveled at night when my relatives would tell me that they weren't going my way and couldn't take me home. I will be totally transparent and admit that I really hated having to travel back home from church by myself.

It was scary being a female teenager traveling the streets of Philadelphia by myself. I tried to be super observant of my surroundings and I walked very fast to get to my destination, being careful not to walk too close to homes where I could be pulled inside or too close to cars driving by. Many times, however, Pastor Blassingame would tell me to get in the car with him and his family and he would take me home. This was a huge inconvenience for him because he lived all the way in the Mt. Airy section of Philadelphia, so I tried to make sure I wasn't a nuisance. He would also make sure I had something to eat on Sundays when my mother didn't have money to give me for dinner after church. I would watch church members (including my own family members) bring food to warm up after church while I had nothing. It was very awkward for me, and I tried not to look out of place, often times going upstairs to the main sanctuary or outside while people ate their food. He was so gracious to me during those very difficult times in my life, especially when the people who were supposed to love me didn't care to look out for me, even though they knew my home situation.

There were not a lot of people who took the time to nurture me during those years of my mother's addiction. I was inwardly praying for some type of emotional connection, support, guidance or affirmation. I was coming into womanhood without a map, very little framework, and no leadership. Most of what I learned, I learned from observation. There were many examples of what not to do, however, I longed for someone to embrace me and help me navigate the world that was waiting for me.

I had a strong desire to attend an out-of-state college and pursue a degree in Early Childhood Education to become a teacher. However, all I could see were numerous obstacles in my path. Given my challenging home life, I couldn't fathom how I would find the financial means to attend college out of state, let alone manage the commute between campus and home. I felt utterly alone in this endeavor, with no one to provide financial assistance. The thought of being stranded on campus during holidays due to lack of support weighed heavily on my mind. During my senior year, I visited Bradford Business School and familiarized myself with their secretarial science program. I was intrigued by the possibility of graduating their certificate program in just ten months and securing a stable job. Nobody had informed me about scholarships, college work-study programs, or how to manage college expenses while working part-time. There was no one to offer encouragement or guide me towards taking a leap of faith and pursuing a college education. A month after graduating from CAPA in 1984, I enrolled at Bradford, feeling like it was my only choice.

   I recall telling my English teacher, Mrs. Pritchett, that I was going to business school instead of college. She was so disappointed! Mrs. Pritchett would make me come to class early sometimes and she would give me a separate reading list. She then expected me to give my thoughts on the books after class. At the time I was livid! Why is this lady giving me extra work??? Why is she singling me out? However, looking back, I realize that she saw potential in me that I wasn't aware of at the time. While she didn't hide her displeasure with my decision, she also didn't know about my difficult home life and the challenges I was facing. I grew up in an era where parents told their kids, "Whatever goes on in this house, stays in this house." You didn't go off and air dirty laundry about what happened in your home. And I didn't! Not to family, not to church members, and certainly not to teachers. I often wonder how Mrs. Pritchett would have reacted if I had told her that I wanted to go to college but didn't know how to deal with my drug-addicted mother and her boyfriend.

After graduating Bradford Business School as a secretary, it opened many doors for employment. There were always secretarial jobs available. I typed around seventy-five words per minute and did Gregg shorthand at one hundred thirty words per minute. I was very employable! After a few secretarial job explorations, I ultimately landed a job at Colonial Penn Life Insurance Company on Market Street downtown. I had a good salary with benefits, and I was super excited to have a "real job!" I paid my mother $200 a month. She was still working for the podiatrist and Be Cool was working at the waterfront in South Philly, which was a very lucrative job. Our rent was around $200 a month so my little contribution should have surely taken care of that.

I was baffled to one day learn that we were being evicted from the apartment and that she and Be Cool were looking for another place to stay. Apparently, they hadn't been paying the rent as I assumed. I was determined to part ways at this point, so I was on the hunt to get away from my mother and her boyfriend AND their drug habit!

Philly was crazy at this time in the 80's. The crack epidemic was in full swing, and many families were basically torn apart. Mothers (and fathers) had abandoned their kids, leaving aging grandmothers the arduous task of raising the next generation. Then there were the children who found themselves, of no fault of their own, motherless, fatherless, and in many instances, hopeless. I counted myself among the fortunate few. I had reached an age where self-sufficiency was within my grasp. With employment secured, I had the autonomy to shape my own destiny through the choices I made and not those made for me by others. It made leaving my mother and Be Cool the easiest and best option for me.

It just so happened that one of my uncle's former girlfriends, Sydney, whom I always liked, also worked at Colonial Penn. I still called her Aunt Sydney and would occasionally go to the floor she worked on to say hello and talk for a few minutes. She knew about my situation with my mother and when I told her we were being evicted, she offered for me to stay at her home with her and her daughter, Topeka. It was a three-story house in North

Philly, not far from where my mother and I used to live with Bobbie. I stayed in the third floor which had a nice sized bedroom, a bathroom, (a kitchenette which was inoperable), and a sitting room, almost like a little living room. It was perfect for me, and I graciously accepted.

Well before eviction day, I packed up my things and parted ways with my mother. I finally felt like I was in control of my own destiny and didn't have to be the recipient of anyone else's bad choices. And it felt great! I was about 18 years old at this time and while I was looking forward to a fresh beginning, it was the beginning of a very dark period in my mother's life as she fell deeper into her addiction. The scars that would form for both of us would last for a very long time to come, further plunging our relationship into a downward spiral. And to be totally honest and transparent, we never recovered even to this day.

I don't think I fully felt the magnitude of being fatherless until my teen and young adult years. Those years I desperately needed guidance and protection. It was difficult navigating life without the support and love of a father. In the back of my mind were always countless questions about these two "fathers" that I supposedly had, but neither stepped up nor stayed in my life. Even Block chose to disappear out of my life after he and my mother split. I remember having to hunt him down so I could have someone walk me down the aisle when I got married. These rejections still haunt me to this day. Even the love of my Savior and my wonderful husband hasn't been able to fully erase the residue of rejection and abandonment.

WORD GIRLZ

"I have loved you with an everlasting love; I have drawn you with unfailing kindness." - Jeremiah 31:3

It's easy to become disheartened when we encounter indifference, betrayal, or neglect from those who we thought cared for us. However, even in these trying times, God's love shines through. The Bible reminds us in Jeremiah 31:3, "I have loved you with an everlasting love; I have drawn you with unfailing kindness." This verse serves as a powerful testament to God's enduring love that surpasses any human limitations.

When faced with adversity, it's natural to question our worth and whether we are deserving of love. But God's promise to never leave us nor forsake us (Deuteronomy 31:6) reaffirms that we are cherished beyond measure. His guidance is the hope that we need as it leads us through the storms, providing strength and resilience even in the face of challenges.

One of the most remarkable aspects of God's love is how it empowers us to extend compassion even to those who have caused us pain. Matthew 5:44 teaches us, "But I tell you, love your enemies and pray for those who persecute you." By showing kindness and forgiveness to those who have harmed us, we become vessels of God's love and exemplify His boundless compassion for all humanity.

God has a remarkable way of using our pain and struggles to bring forth blessings in our lives and in the lives of those around us. Romans 8:28 assures us, "And we know that in all things God works for the good of those who love him, who have been called according to his purpose." Our hardships become opportunities for growth, empathy, and a deeper understanding of the human experience, allowing us to shine a light in the midst of darkness.

By extending love to those who have hurt us, we reflect the very essence of God's love for humanity. As we navigate through life's trials, we can rest assured that our pain will not be in vain – for God can turn it into a source of blessings and healing for ourselves and others.

top row: Classmates Kim, Marie, and Jennifer. Bottom row: Candie and Tanya. One thing for sure, I always smiled for the camera! When I look at this picture of my high school friends and me, I know for sure that this was taken our senior year. What they didn't know was that my senior year was also the beginning of my mom's drug addiction, part of the reason why I couldn't afford a school shirt to wear in this picture. It's funny how you can be around people every day, yet they never know what you're going through. I've talked to several high school friends recently and each one of them told me that they remember my sunny disposition and pleasant attitude and would never have guessed what I was living through. All I know is that God remained faithful to me despite my circumstances, and also we can become masters at hiding what's really going on!

Although I was proud to have graduated high school, something my mother had not, I was scared. I didn't see college as an option because of finances and lack of information (no one told me about scholarships, military, or trade schools), and honestly, I just saw my home life as getting worse and not better (and I was right)! I decided to go to Bradford Business School and take up secretarial science so that I would always have a "good job!" I see now that God's delay isn't denial and I was about to see how He was masterminding my life from the background.

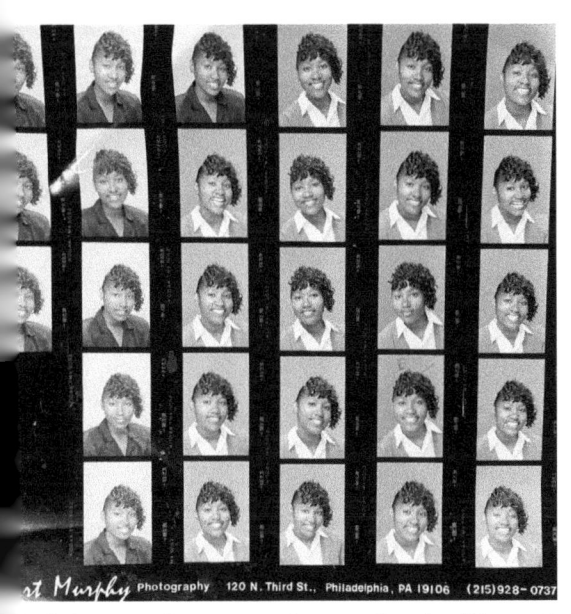

Fun fact about me: I auditioned for The Cosby Show. I attended The Philadelphia High School for the Creative and Performing Arts (CAPA) as a creative writing major, although I could also sing and wanted to act. CAPA was fairly new when I attended and cross-training in other majors wasn't instituted yet. So, I sometimes got to sing gospel with the vocal majors after school our senior year. But after high school, I took an acting class with Fame's Carlo Imperato (Danny) at Locust Street Theater in West Philadelphia and took theater and movement classes at Freedom Theater in North Philadelphia. While at Freedom Theater, attendees were invited to audition for The Cosby Show as they were looking for performers to play friends to the Huxtable kids. I performed a piece by Sonia Sanchez (a fact I shared with her when she visited the church in 2009). These pictures are from my professional acting portfolio. We all know that I didn't get a part, but it was a great experience, nonetheless. Nothing beats a failure but a try (truly the only piece of advice I can credit my mom for giving me)! I chose to live a life without regrets, seizing any opportunities that would afford me the ability to learn and/or grow. I still live my life that way! I was also trying to find my place in the world. I'm still on that journey.

STRAIGHT OUTTA BROKENNESS

CHAPTER 4: ON MY OWN FOR REAL

"You never know which experiences of life are going to be of value ... You've got to leave yourself open to the hidden opportunities."
– Robin Roberts

I stayed at my Aunt Sydney's a little over a year before I moved out of state to Virginia. One of my closest church friends, Wanda Loftlin, had recently married, had a baby and moved to Virginia with her husband, Walter, who had a job opportunity in the Portsmouth, Virginia area. Walter was a great big teddy bear of a guy, and an exceptional chef. Wanda's sister, Sherry, and I thought this would be a great opportunity for us to get out of Philly and get jobs in Virginia. Walter had two other friends who were moving out there as well, so one could say we were going to be like the crew on Living Single and Friends before they were actual shows! Sherry and I moved in with Wanda and Walter and their baby girl. We were close to Virginia Beach and spent some time there, hung out with one another, and began looking for employment. Wanda and Sherry's uncle was a pastor in the area so we worshipped at his church when we could. Everything was fine except one thing: I couldn't find a job paying enough money for my satisfaction. Since we were so close to the military base, the secretarial jobs were low paying since employers believed they could pay military wives next to nothing to do those jobs. I went on several interviews, but the pay was so low, I couldn't stand it. After several months, I resolved to go back to Philly. I left a good paying job and knew that I could acquire another one. I was not about to work as a secretary for five dollars an hour in Virginia when I knew I could make $20k in Philadelphia!

I hated leaving my friends, and I was sad that my adventure to a new state didn't pan out as I had hoped, but I had to look out for myself. I was the first one to leave. Sherry wasn't far behind me and some years later Wanda would also follow with her two young daughters after Walter's untimely death.

When I came back to Philly, I didn't go back to Aunt Sydney's. My god sister Sharron's mother, Dorothy Brown, offered a room at her house on 8th and Susquehanna and I stayed there for a few months while an apartment was being prepared for me around the corner from my church at 19th and Susquehanna. The apartment was in one of two buildings owned by our church and my pastor, Rev. A. T. Blassingame, made sure it was ready for me. There were also a few other members and their families who lived in the second building. One thing for sure, I was never late for church!

I was really on my own this time. I had to learn how to get utilities turned on in my name, how to manage my money, pay my bills on time, how to buy furniture, etc., all the things no one took the time to teach me. I had to learn on my own or recall from memory what I watched my mom, or others do throughout the years.

I didn't have much communication with my mother. I remember her calling me one time for money for food. I told her that I couldn't give her money, but that she could come by and get food. She arrived at my doorstep, and I gave her almost all of the food that was in my fridge and freezer (I had just gone food shopping). I didn't see her again for a while after that and really had no idea where she was living or how she was doing. She was well into her addiction now and I knew it was actually better for me to shelter my heart from the dark abyss of her struggles.

While I enjoyed the sanctuary that I built for myself - a drama-free, drug-free home, I was lonely. Yes, I went to work. Yes, I went to church and hung out with friends sometimes, but I was lonely. Living alone was fine until it wasn't. I hadn't taken the time to figure out what I liked and didn't like, or what my interests really were because my life had always been about responding to what was happening around me or to me. I wish someone had told me that I should have been taking that time to discover and explore what I truly wanted in my life, that I should get to know ME for the first time, perhaps the experience of living alone would have been different and more rewarding. I had a boyfriend at the time, and we were off and on for almost three years. I knew that the relationship was going nowhere, but I held on for as long as I could because it was something to hold on to.

At this point, I was working as an Administrative Assistant in the Registrar's Office at Temple Law School. I've had quite a few jobs in the past, and I've often left them for better opportunities. Whenever I felt dissatisfied with how I was treated or if I found a job offering a higher salary elsewhere, I would update my resume and move on. Throughout my life, I've experienced a pattern of moving around and instability, mostly stemming from my childhood or circumstances beyond my control. It took me a while to realize that some of my moves were a result of my willingness to escape from situations or people that didn't benefit my well-being. If I were to self-analyze, I'd say that I wanted to avoid being forced into situations, as I was in my childhood, where I wasn't valued or appreciated. Having said that, I wish someone had taught me how to commit and persevere, how to manage my emotions and expectations, and how to establish the stability I clearly longed for in my life. Those skills eventually came, but it took some time!

Working at Temple Law School was a fantastic experience. I worked in the Registrar's Office, and my boss, the registrar, Barbara Bennett Yates, was truly amazing. She was not only welcoming and pleasant but also an inspiring figure as the first Black female boss I had ever worked under. Barbara exuded class, strength, confidence, and kindness, and I held her in high esteem.

My time at Temple Law School ended up being more meaningful than I would ever imagine. My church and apartment were conveniently located not far from the school, and a few Temple University students had learned about our church from a cafeteria worker who was a church member. These students occasionally joined us for worship, and I got to know them and started to hang out with them frequently, even inviting them to my apartment for get togethers. They introduced me to a campus ministry called

Bridge the Gap, which was comprised of other young adults who loved the Lord and wanted to grow in Him. This ministry had two main components: a weeknight Bible study held in the athletic dorms (which I initially attended) and a larger group that met on Friday afternoons. Since I worked on campus, I started going to the Friday afternoon Bible studies and quickly formed strong connections with the amazing group of young people who gathered each week. They were genuinely devoted to their faith, and our Bible studies were inspiring. We worshiped together, delved into the Scriptures, and then spent hours fellowshipping at restaurants or someone's apartment. Bridge the Gap not only led me to lifelong friendships, but it also changed the trajectory of my life during a time when I had no clear plan or idea of where my life was headed, and definitely no guidance to help me figure it out.

My home church was filled with children and young adults when I was growing up, but by this time in my life many of the young people my age had stopped coming to church, either because their parents changed memberships or they stopped going to church altogether. I didn't have a whole lot of people to hang out with so Bridge the Gap was right on time. I still went to my church on Sunday mornings, but if there was a Bridge the Gap fellowship, either during the week or on the weekends, I made it a point to go.

Bridge the Gap was founded by Temple student, Troy A. Bronner, who, after graduating, was moving to Rochester, NY with his new bride, Jill, to attend Colgate Rochester Divinity School. Troy left the ministry in the hands of Donald Graves, Curtis Morris, and others as he prepared to move. Both Donald and Curtis became like family to me. Donald was cheerful and fun to be around, and we often enjoyed meals together as he was still a student, and I worked on campus. Curtis, on the other hand, assumed the role of a protective big brother in my life. He frequently scolded me for my on-again, off-again relationship with my boyfriend of nearly three years.

Curtis would say, "You need to let that loser go," but I would just laugh it off. Deep down, I knew he wasn't entirely wrong, but I held onto hope, even though the signs were there. My boyfriend was five years older than I and came from a large family known for their musical talents. They often performed at churches across the city. Interestingly, I had been friends with his older sister before we started dating. She had warned me not to get involved with him, but at the time, I brushed it off as her being overly critical. This led to a huge fight between her and my boyfriend, resulting in a strained relationship between me and his sister.

My boyfriend had a beautiful voice, and made me laugh, however, his tendency towards jealousy was a turn-off and I couldn't envision what a life with him would look like. He didn't seem particularly passionate about anything or ever spoke about life goals or what he aspired to do with his life. Looking back, I think I was more in love with the idea of being in love than being in love with him. One day, after church, he unexpectedly showed up. I was chatting with one of my friends who had casually put his arm around me just as my boyfriend approached. He was clearly upset and asked aggressively, "Who is that guy?" I tried to defuse the situation, saying, "Calm down, he's just a friend. Let's go to my place." However, once inside my apartment, he lost his temper completely.

He interrogated me about the guy with his arm around me, and I couldn't believe his jealousy. I explained that he was a friend from my church and nothing more. Despite my attempts to calm the situation, he grew increasingly furious and eventually reached over and yanked off the gold chain I was wearing, which had his name on it. That moment triggered something in me, perhaps memories of my mother's past experiences with abuse or the "Larry" incident. In any case, it wasn't pretty. I walked to the kitchen and returned with a butcher knife in my hand, shouting, "Don't you ever put your hands on me!"

He was taken aback, not expecting my reaction. "I didn't put my hands on you," he said holding the chain in between his fingers. "Get out! Get out!" I hollered at him. He didn't know what to say or do, so he left.

I stored that incident in the back of my mind, vowing never to forget it. It was the most explosive encounter we ever had. We had normal boyfriend-girlfriend spats before, but nothing like that. The fact that it was the second time I had used a knife in a confrontation with a grown man wasn't lost on me. I had a vision of the person I wanted to become and the life I desired to live, and God and I both knew this wasn't it. It forced me to remember a time when my mother and Be Cool argued about drugs. I was in my room, and they were in their room, but the argument spilled into mine (remember they had to pass through my room to get to theirs). Be Cool grabbed my mother, seemingly ready to strike her. I can't explain where I found the strength, but I wrapped my arms around him from behind, lifted him up, and turned him away from her, shouting, "Don't even think about putting your hands on my mother!" Both were high and wandered off after that incident. When they left my room, I stood in the middle of my floor and declared to myself and to God, "I will NEVER be like her!" That promise became my purpose from that point onward. I would not follow my mother's mistakes, nor would I choose the type of partners she chose.

After that incident, my boyfriend and I broke up, and I was determined to live my best life. I went to work, attended Bridge the Gap, went to church, and returned home unbothered by our latest breakup. We must have been broken up for several months because a lot happened in the interim.

One night, while I was sound asleep in my bedroom, the Holy Spirit woke me up and urged me to turn on the light. In a groggy state, I reached up and switched on the light just before a man was about to climb through my bedroom window. He had already removed the television and all the stuffed animals I had placed above and around it. The sudden light startled him, and he quickly fled. I couldn't believe that someone had nearly broken into my apartment! My immediate reaction was to call my Pastor, shouting, "I have to get out of here!" Church members who lived in the neighboring building heard the commotion of him running in the alley and called to check if I was okay. I am continuously thankful for God's protection that night.

The next day I began my search for a new apartment. Honestly, it was a bit nerve-wracking to be apartment hunting on my own. My first apartment had been provided by the church, as a result I hadn't needed to go through formal rental procedures. This was one of those times when

I felt alone and had to navigate things by myself. I didn't have time to wallow or feel sorry for what or who I didn't have. I had to put on my big girl panties and figure it out just like I did every other time.

Eventually, I found an affordable apartment located at 4408 Sansom Street in West Philadelphia. I vividly recall the day I went to view the apartment; the landlord had arranged a tour with the current tenant. Her kindness left a lasting impression on me. She shared all the things she loved about the apartment and the neighborhood, which gave me a sense of comfort. I believe she was a lawyer, though I can't remember why she was moving. Nevertheless, she had only positive things to say about the landlord and her experience living there. That day, I decided to secure the apartment before someone else could.

Some friends from Bridge the Gap helped me with the move, and I settled into this spacious one-bedroom apartment. It was on the first floor again, but it had windows with security bars that strangely made me feel safe along with the key code entry system on the front door. I adored the apartment with its large bay windows, two floor-to-ceiling sliding doors that separated the living room from my bedroom, a decent-sized bathroom, and a full-sized kitchen. I also had access to the basement, which I only used for storage. Two other apartments occupied the second and third floors, and my neighbors were quiet and considerate. I had no problems during my time there.

I had been at 4408 for several months before one of my church members, Sheila, needed a place to stay. I had known Sheila for a long time, so I didn't hesitate to offer that she be my roommate. However, I was smart enough to know that she would need to be equally responsible for the rent and utilities. I contacted the landlord, and he added Sheila to the apartment lease. Since it was a one-bedroom apartment, we got two daybeds and put them in the bedroom, and we split all the bills down the middle. It was nice having someone in the apartment with me, I really didn't prefer to live alone.

One day, while I was at Bridge the Gap, I discussed the idea of going bowling for my birthday with Curtis. He agreed to join me, along with Sheila. As we were chatting, Arthur Price, a friend to Curtis and one of the guys who led devotional sessions, approached us. Curtis introduced him and suggested, "Art, you should join us for bowling to celebrate Candie's birthday." Arthur had a dark complexion, wore glasses, and always looked well-groomed. He stood at about 5 feet 7 inches tall with a slender build. "Of course you should come," I said. Thus, the plans were set for my birthday bowling outing. However, Curtis had to cancel, leaving Arthur, Sheila, and me to go on the outing together.

We went bowling and had dinner afterward. While observing them, I couldn't help but think they would make a cute couple. To be honest I came to that conclusion because Arthur was not very tall, and Sheila was not even 5 feet. It became clear to me, eventually, that Arthur was not interested in Sheila and I didn't push the idea. Arthur and I became good friends after that evening. It wasn't unusual for me to have male friends, as I had more male friends than female ones throughout the years. I got along well with guys; they either saw me as a little sister or a female friend they trusted. One guy even told me, "You're the marrying kind," implying that I was the type of girl you marry, not date casually. I know what he meant and appreciated the compliment. It was also nice to be around guys who were actual friends and not trying to sleep with me!

My ex called me and expressed a desire to get back together. We made a date for him to visit my new apartment. To my surprise, he arrived with a marriage proposal and a ring! I was taken aback and didn't know how to react. Should I take him back? Was he serious? He had a ring and was saying all the right things. I had invested almost three years of my life into our relationship. Despite not feeling overwhelmed with excitement, I said yes, and what followed would become a story for the ages! One thing for sure, I was about to find out how important it is to be open to the leading of the Holy Spirit.

WORD GIRLZ

And we know that in all things, God works for the good of those who love Him, who have been called according to His purpose. - Romans 8:28

In this journey of life, we often find ourselves at crossroads, faced with decisions that can shape our destinies. It's during these pivotal moments that many of us turn to our faith and seek God's guidance. As believers, we firmly believe that God orders our steps, leading us down the path that aligns with His divine plan.

One of the fundamental aspects of walking in God's will is learning to listen to the Holy Spirit. The Holy Spirit is our divine counselor and guide, constantly speaking to our hearts and minds. It is through prayer, meditation on Scripture, and quiet moments of reflection that we can discern His voice. Proverbs 3:6 reminds us, "In all your ways acknowledge Him, and He shall direct your paths." When we acknowledge God in our decision-making process and actively seek His guidance, we position ourselves to receive His direction.

We must be open to God's direction which means surrendering our own plans and desires to His perfect will. This can be challenging at times, especially when God's guidance seems to lead us in a different direction than we initially intended. However, it's important to remember that God's ways are higher than ours, and His perspective is infinitely more profound. Isaiah 55:8-9 reminds us, "For my thoughts are not your thoughts, neither are your ways my ways, declares the Lord."

When we are open to God's direction, we demonstrate our trust in His wisdom and sovereignty. It's crucial to release our fears and doubts into His capable hands and have faith that His plan for our lives is far greater than anything we could imagine.

Romans 8:28 assures us, "And we know that in all things, God works for the good of those who love Him, who have been called according to His purpose." This verse is a powerful reminder that even in the midst of challenging circumstances and unexpected detours, God is always working for our good. His love for us is unwavering, and His plans for our lives are designed to mold us into the image of Christ.

Sometimes, it may seem like God's direction leads us through valleys of hardship or uncertainty. However, it's in these moments that we must remember that God's ultimate goal is to bring glory to Himself through our lives. As we trust His guidance and walk in obedience, our testimonies become a powerful reflection of His grace and faithfulness.

II. PUZZLE PIECES

CHAPTER 5: Prince Charming Comes Anyway

"Where there is love there is life."
– Mahatma Gandhi

Is there anything crazier than a man putting a ring on your finger and then disappearing for two weeks? Yes, you read that correctly! My ex put a ring on my finger and then he disappeared for two weeks! Remember during this time, there is no social media - no Facebook or Instagram to spy on to see where he is or who he's with! There are no cell phones - no way to text, "Hey, where are you?" Just landlines and broken promises! Before we get to all of that, let's discuss what happened in the two weeks during his disappearing act.

After the proposal I started slipping out to folks that I was engaged - after all, there was a ring on my finger. Now mind you, Arthur Price and I were becoming good friends, and we talked often on the phone, but I had not yet told him about the return of the ex or the ring on my finger. First, before you get the wrong impression of our relationship or of me, let me clarify something. Arthur and I were JUST friends. However, I'm not stupid. I had a feeling that he would have liked to be more than friends. He didn't come out and say it, but I had a feeling. I didn't see him in that way and I made sure that my interaction with him was purely platonic. Remember, I had plenty of guy friends and I knew how to be "just their friend!"

One Friday after Bridge the Gap Bible Study, I was talking to a friend who had just found out that I was engaged. He came over to me very bubbly and said, "Congratulations on your engagement," just as Arthur was approaching. I will never forget the look on his face, and I immediately felt bad and awkward because I hadn't had the opportunity to tell him myself. Being the gentleman that he is, he said, "Congratulations," and then proceeded to ask if he could speak to me in the hallway. I followed him into the hallway, and he said, "I just wanted to say that I wish you the best on your engagement and I pray everything works out for you." Ohhhhh, how sweet! I thanked him and that was that! We rejoined everyone inside, and folks began to give me their best wishes. If people could see how I felt inside! I felt like a fraud! Who has a ring on her finger and can't find her fiancé? At this point, he had been AWOL for at least four or five days. I wasn't the happy bride-to-be that I should have been, and it made me sick to my stomach standing in front of everyone pretending that I was. I knew it was a mistake to take him back! Honestly, I was over him! Even the proposal itself wasn't the tear at your heartstrings, I love you so much, kind of proposal. It was lackluster at best, and I can't even remember what he said!

Ladies, when you know something is over, go with your gut! Don't be in love with the idea of being in love! Don't be in love with the idea of being married! If the love "don't fit, you must acquit!" MOVE ON and be alright with it!

When I got home alone with my thoughts, I just cried out to God to fix it! I didn't want to be with anyone whom I wasn't supposed to be with! If this relationship is not what He wants for my life, then let this man STAY GONE!!! I wanted to please God with my life, and I trusted Him with my heart! I told the Lord that I was content with Him and that I didn't need any relationship, especially if it wasn't going to honor Him and it wasn't going to make me feel loved FOR REAL. I also didn't believe that I would ever get married or find someone who would treat me the way

I knew I deserved to be treated! Look at my examples! There weren't many marriages that I looked at that gave me much hope! I resolved to just being content by myself and honoring God with my life!

Well, not only did God hear my prayers, but the Enemy heard them also! In that two-week period, it seemed that every guy I knew came out the woodwork! Suddenly there was this "interest" in me that hadn't been there before. One guy (I don't even know HOW he got my number) called me to tell me that The LORD told him that I was going to be his wife, which I know was ridiculous because I know he wasn't attracted to women! I kindly told him to tell the Lord to relay that to me!!!! The nerve!!! What a crazy two weeks! I honestly felt like I was under Satanic attack! Something wasn't right about all of this, and it just made me pray harder! I wasn't interested in any of these guys, and I just wanted to be left alone. It felt like a set-up by the enemy, and I wasn't falling for it! I didn't even want my ex to come back - I was over it and I didn't shed one tear over him.

I kindly declined the crazy offers and settled into the mindset of being saved, single, and satisfied. Until the ex showed up at my door.

It had been a full two weeks, and my door rang. I walked to the door and lo and behold he was standing there as if I just saw him the day before. Well, I was young, and good and petty back then so the first thing out of my mouth was, "Can I help you?" Before he could muster a word or an explanation or anything, I told him, "Hold on one minute!" I closed the door, went into my room, retrieved the ring, returned to the door, opened it, and gave the ring back!

"Can we talk about this?" he said.

I emphatically replied, "There's nothing to talk about! It's obvious that this isn't going to work, so here's your ring. There's nothing left to say!"

And that, my friend, was the end of that! For years I felt like I should have at least let him explain, mostly out of curiosity, but truthfully, it wouldn't have mattered. That relationship was no good for me, and he was no good for me. I had enough of people not choosing me, not appreciating me, not seeing ME, especially when I loved hard and unconditionally! Consequently, I walked away and didn't look back. Years later I would learn that the probable reason why he disappeared was because he had gotten someone pregnant. Yes. A hot mess! So grateful I removed myself from that situation.

Now here I am no longer a fiancé, and not in the least bit sad about it! I would do as I told the Lord I would do: concentrate on my relationship with Him. I went back to my usual routine: work, church, and Bridge the Gap!

Eventually word got out that I was no longer engaged.

It was inevitable. Folks began to ask questions about the wedding, etc., and I was open and honest. "We broke up and I am fine," was my reply.

One day after Bridge the Gap Bible Study, Arthur came up to me while I was talking to someone. We hadn't talked since the congratulations incident (he was being respectful of my relationship) and I hadn't reached out to him. I thought it would be a little weird if I were to call him and say, "Hey, how are you? I'm no longer engaged." So, I just left it alone. When he approached me, he said, "Hey, can I have a word with you for a minute?" I said sure and followed him into the hallway. I remember thinking to myself, "What was it with this guy and the hallway?"

Once in the hallway, he looks at me and says, "I heard that you are no longer engaged."

I replied, "Yeah. We broke up."

He then looked at me with this serious glare and said, "Well, I just want you to know that I know the Lord told me that you are going to be my wife, and I want you to know that I'm not going anywhere!"

He then turned around and left me standing there with my mouth wide open. In that very moment it was like I saw him in a different light, and it immediately took my breath away! I felt like Diana Ross in Lady Sings the Blues when Billy Dee Williams said," Do you want my arm to fall off?"

Now let's get something straight, this was not the same type of "God told me…" that I heard from that guy during the ex's two-week disappearing act! This "God told me…" had some power behind it and so much swag! It surprised me, yet it intrigued me. It felt….. genuine! After I picked my mouth up from the floor, I walked back into the room feeling like I had just been swept off my feet and from that day on, Arthur Price and I became inseparable.

    I would be remiss if I didn't share with you the backstory behind Arthur's Billy Dee Williams swag! Apparently, when I showed up engaged, he was devastated. He called his spiritual mother in disbelief because he knew what he heard God say to him; that I was THE ONE! During this time, Bridge the Gap founder, Troy Bronner and his wife, Jill, were moving to Rochester, New York from Philadelphia so that he could attend Colgate Rochester Divinity School. Arthur went on the road trip with them to help them move. Legend has it that Arthur wouldn't stop talking about me on the five-hour drive to Rochester. He couldn't believe how wrong he had been! When he found out that I was no longer engaged, he was not going to let me slip away again. Now isn't that the most beautiful love story?

    Arthur was a breath of fresh air! We were already friends so getting to know each other even more was so easy!

He was such a gentleman: opening doors for me, buying flowers, taking me out to very nice restaurants. When I say he wined and dined me, believe me. Most of all, we thoroughly enjoyed talking about everything, especially our faith! I was heavily involved in ministry at my church and so was he at his church. We both had a passion for youth ministry! I loved pouring into the youth at my church; so much so, that I was prone to have weekend sleepovers at my apartment to give parents a break and to pour biblical wisdom into the youth. I would also hold afternoon services to reward them for their report cards and took the A/B honor roll students on outings.

Arthur was a gifted Bible Study teacher and mentor to young people at his church. He was so revered that one of his former Sunday School students, Tariq Trotter (you might know him as Black Thought from The Roots), wrote about him fondly in his book, The Upclycled Self. It was so refreshing to be with someone who loved ministry as I did, and we would later decide that doing ministry together was a strong desire for us both.

Arthur asked me out for Valentine's Day, 1988. He took me to a beautiful, classy, restaurant overlooking Philadelphia and nine days later on February 23, 1988, he asked me to be his girlfriend. It was official - we were exclusive. I'm sure to others we looked like an unlikely pair! Arthur seemed very conservative. He worked at the Philadelphia District Attorney's Office as a Prosecution Assistant, and he wore a suit and tie EVERY day! He always looked serious and rather pensive, but others didn't know how much he made me laugh! I, on the other hand, was probably seen as the girl around the way - a little fly and a little loud!

On paper we were probably opposites. I admit that he wasn't as tall as the guys I had dated, and the suit and tie every day was a little stuffier than I was used to. He wasn't what I considered my usual "type." For some reason I was enamored with the tall, lighter skinned guys who had a little edge. Not necessarily bad boys- because I didn't want a bad boy - they didn't know how to treat women, in my opinion. But one thing I learned, thank God, is that you can close yourself off and miss the blessing God has for you if you pigeonhole yourself into a certain "type." "Types" are superficial at best and rarely involve seeing and loving someone for who they are. I immediately let that stupid list go and opened my heart to the possibility of being with Arthur Price, Jr. He was my wavy haired, chocolate drop and I'm so glad I listened to the Spirit!

Arthur was so smart! This Dude graduated high school in three years instead of four and got accepted into Temple University as a Criminal Justice major, the first in his immediate family to get a four-year degree. I was in awe of his intelligence, and it really inspired me to enroll at Temple with his full support and encouragement. I began classes at Temple in August of 1989. We would often meet on campus after my classes and grab a bite to eat or hang out. One day after classes, Arthur picked me up from campus and we headed to one of our favorite restaurants, Rib-It's, to get some ribs. He proposed to me that day, September 11, 1989, and I happily said yes!

We didn't believe in long engagements, and we soon settled on a date for just eight months later, May 19, 1990. We were babies - he was 24 and I was 23. Our daughters often talk about how young we were and how we would never have let them marry so early. They are correct! It was a different time! Many of our friends were getting married also, it wasn't uncommon, especially in the Christian community. If you didn't want to "live in sin," you got married! Now, I am a little "old school" and I still think you should get married rather than "live in sin," but I think young people today want to explore more of life before they settle down and get married.

Our wedding was absolutely beautiful! The entire week before I was so sick, and it rained most of the week. I really believe it was nerves that attacked my immune system. At any rate, on the day of our wedding it was a gorgeous day.

I was also cool as a cucumber, which allowed me to really enjoy the day and savor each moment. It was about 75 degrees outside with a gentle breeze and no remnant of the rain that had transpired the week before. We got married at Grace Baptist Church of Germantown in front of three hundred and fifty friends and family. Arthur and I paid for our own wedding and my aunt, Irene, and family members did the catering for the reception. We wanted our wedding to really mean something, so we decided that it should mirror a church service - something that represented us. We would feel cheated to spend a ton of money on a wedding, only for the ceremony to be twenty minutes long. Troy Bronner delivered a rousing sermon (When the Wedding Becomes a Marriage), and we had Cooke Junior High School Alumni Choir and Wendell Miller, a wonderful and well-known soloist, provide the choir selections. Folks still talk about our wedding ceremony to this day!

Mahatma Gandhi said, "When there is love, there is life," and it's true! Arthur showered me with unconditional love - something I had never experienced from a human before and it was life-changing! Not only did he love me, but he let me see that I was worthy of being loved. He opened the window for me to see what it was like to be wanted and adored and I will always be grateful to him for that. Our marriage isn't perfect, we are imperfect people, but we continue to be committed to each other despite our flaws, our differences, or our upbringing. God remains the glue that has kept us together for thirty four years and I am forever grateful that both of us listened to the Holy Spirit on that day after Bible Study. We were crafted for each other before the foundation of the world and even though we didn't know it then, we were about to embark on the ride of our lives…. Together!

WORD GIRLZ

Love is patient, love is kind. It does not envy, it does not boast, it is not proud. It does not dishonor others, it is not self-seeking, it is not easily angered, it keeps no record of wrongs. Love does not delight in evil but rejoices with the truth. It always protects, always trusts, always hopes, always perseveres. Love never fails. And now these three remain: faith, hope and love. But the greatest of these is love. -I Corinthians 13: 4-8;13

I Corinthians 13 is the scripture that became the foundation for our wedding day. It was the scripture upon which we based the vows we wrote to one another. It is often referred to as the "Love Chapter," and is a heartfelt exposition of love by the Apostle Paul. In this chapter, Paul emphasizes that without love, all our actions and achievements are meaningless. This verse reminds us that love should be the foundation of our words and actions in any relationship, especially in marriage. Love is not just about romantic gestures but the way we speak to and treat one another daily. We will all have trials and challenges in our relationships with others. However, it is during these times that love is tested and 1 Peter 4:8 (ESV) encourages us to maintain love amidst difficulties: "Above all, keep loving one another earnestly since love covers a multitude of sins."

Romans 12:12 (ESV) reminds us to remain hopeful and patient in trying times: "Rejoice in hope, be patient in tribulation, be constant in prayer." Love that endures through hardships strengthens the bond of those in relationship with one another and demonstrates true commitment.

As we apply these biblical principles, we can build strong, enduring, and Christ-centered relationships that reflect the love of God Himself.

Arthur and Candie. I believe we were engaged at this time..

(l-r) Gary "Block" Townsell (my stepfather), Diane Tribble (my mother), Candie and Arthur, Juanita Price (Arthur's mother), and Arthur Price, Sr., (Arthur's father) May 19, 1990.

Our wedding day will go down in history as a love story for the ages! Some folks didn't understand why a loud, fly girl and seemingly quiet guy would wind up together (we actually got a book about opposites attracting as a gift, so I know it was being talked about!) It wasn't your traditional wedding, by any means. The Dude and I had made the conscious decision to turn our wedding into an actual service, complete with choir and a sermon. Folks thought we were crazy when we tried to explain how the day would go, but they still reminisce about our unique wedding to this day! Cooke Jr. High School reunion choir and Rev. Wendell Miller graced us with their vocal brilliance and set the tone for a service of worship! Both of our pastors, Rev. Charles Walker and Rev. Albert Blassingame were the officiants and Rev. Troy Bronner preached the still memorable sermon- "When the wedding becomes a marriage." Time stood still on that day while we both lovingly vowed to stick together through thick and thin, til death do us part.. He will always be "The Dude" for me.

CHAPTER 6: Motherhood from the Motherless

About the expression "Hurt people, hurt people".. Hurt people are not going to stop HURTING other people until they receive the memo that it is WRONG, (or if there are actual consequences for their behavior.) Feeling sorry for them and understanding where they 'came from' is not helping to stop the cycle of abuse."
-Darlene Ouimet

The Dude and I settled into our lives as newlyweds with ease. The only issue at the time was where we would go to worship. I was a member of Faith Tabernacle Holiness Church in North Philadelphia, and he belonged to 19th Street Baptist Church in South Philadelphia. I had reservations about attending 19th Street because I was hearing rumors about the pastor's divorce, and I just didn't want to go into a situation with a spiritual leader who had that kind of cloud over his ministry. In those days especially, divorce was frowned upon in the Christian community and it just seemed messy to me! It was also assumed that the wife would go worship with her husband to keep the family unit connected. I wasn't having it! After going to separate churches, I decided to take matters into my own hands and find a neutral church we would both feel comfortable attending.

One Sunday I went to worship at Sharon Baptist Church in West Philadelphia, under the leadership of Pastor Keith Reed. Pastor Reed was well known in the city and his church was absolutely the place to be! I had visited many times and even attended a few Women's Bible studies. We also knew several people from Bridge the Gap who were members, so it just seemed like the perfect alternative for our church dilemma. My goal was to approach Pastor Reed after church and get him to agree with me that Sharon was to be our place of worship.

I can't recall exactly what Pastor Reed preached about that Sunday because it has been so long ago, but I know I left that church that day so convicted of my plan, and I clearly heard the Lord tell me to stop my foolishness and join my husband's church. I was devastated! Don't misunderstand, Pastor Walker was an exceptional preacher, and the church service and the congregation were great, I just didn't want to follow a pastor who had been divorced. "How could he, as my spiritual leader, guide my husband and me if he couldn't make it work with his own wife?" were my thoughts. However, one thing about me: if the Lord tells me to do something, I'm going to do it. I don't play with Him like that!

I had to sit with my instructions for a few Sundays before I finally joined. I didn't want the attention on a Sunday morning, so I strategically waited until a Sunday evening service to walk down the aisle.

There are times in your life when God will show you that He knows better than you and your opinions, assumptions, or plans. 19th Street turned out to be the place where we both needed to be. I already had a good biblical foundation at Faith Tabernacle, but I learned so much, grew in my faith, and honed my leadership skills even more at 19th Street.

Six months into our marriage, The Dude felt the call to the preaching ministry and became an Associate Minister. Right after that our friend, the one who introduced us to one another, Curtis Morris, was also called to preach and the two of them were like dynamos on the preaching team! Another fun fact is that I eventually became Pastor Walker's Administrative Assistant and began to work at the church full-time. Yes, God has a way of interrupting your plans for your good and His glory!

The Dude and I both became very involved with 19th Street, while enjoying being newlyweds. We had a great group of friends whom we hung out with regularly and we were both thrilled to be doing ministry together. We had a cute apartment on 5th and Catharine Street, not far from the infamous South Street, and only a few blocks away from The Dude's grandmother's house, where he practically grew up.

On May 5, 1992, two weeks shy of our second wedding anniversary, we welcomed Eboni Paige Price into our lives. I couldn't believe that I was a mother! I had a very pleasant pregnancy, wasn't sick at all, and didn't have a thing to complain about. The Dude was very attentive both during and after pregnancy. He was a very present father to Eboni, and we were anticipating buying a house and settling in with our little family.

We began looking at larger apartments and houses since our current one-bedroom apartment was not going to accommodate our growing family. There was, however, one thing that pretty much made the decision for us. The Dude began to feel God calling him to the pastorate ministry and Rev. Walker started planting seminary into his mind. Troy A. Bronner, founder of Bridge the Gap, and the one who preached at our wedding, was already attending Colgate Rochester Divinity School in Rochester, New York. Pastor Walker was also an alumnus of Colgate, so the fix was in. The Dude, however, was very hesitant to take the plunge to attend seminary. How could we go from a two-income family with a little baby to a no income family? It would surely be a faith walk. After much prayer and deliberation, we decided to pack up our little family and move to Rochester, New York while Eboni was just three months old. Everything happened so fast; we had moved to an unknown place and were about to venture out on an unknown journey that was both frightening and exciting to say the least.

A long way from home, Arthur and I found a church, Mt. Vernon Baptist Church, to attend while living in Rochester. We were taught that if you moved away temporarily, you were to find a church and join under Watch Care. Watch Care just meant that we would be active members of the new church, with the understanding that our primary membership remained at 19th Street Baptist in Philly. Mt. Vernon was a large congregation with many families that made up the church demographics. It was a very welcoming church, and we quickly assimilated into the church culture. The pastor, Rev. J. D. Jackson, embraced Arthur and included him on his ministerial staff without hesitation.

Mt. Vernon didn't treat us like strangers, and we made very meaningful connections there. I can't mention our time in Rochester without lauding two families that meant the most to us: Ms. Deloris Ford and family, and the Franklins.

Ms. Deloris Ford, or "Momma Ford," as we called her, was a wonderful blessing to our lives. She embraced us as if we were her children - always opening her home and making sure that we were loved, received, and fed! Momma Ford had one son, Tony (and his family), and a sister that lived nearby. Tony and his wife, Virginia, had a daughter, Maya, the same age as our little Eboni; it was a wonderful blend of our families. We will be forever grateful for the care in which Momma Ford and her family nurtured and embraced us in this very early stage of our marriage!

The Franklins—Doddie, Darrell, and their two children, Danna and Darren—became our family away from home and a true blessing in our lives. From the moment they first laid eyes on Eboni, they showered her with love and welcomed us into their home with open arms. Their support was unwavering, especially through the heartache of a miscarriage we endured a year after Eboni was born. When we joyously welcomed our rainbow baby, Amyna Janel, into the world on December 11, 1994, they were right there by our side, lovingly embracing their role as her godparents.

Mt. Vernon, in general, was such a loving church to

us and we never had a lonely holiday or important event without receiving several invitations to dine and fellowship. Rochester (though much colder than I would have liked), had the warmest, kindest folks, and we will always look back at those years with fondness.

It is not hard to admit that the love I received from those wonderful mothers, Momma Ford, and Doddie Franklin, helped shape my mothering style in those early stages of being a mother to my girls. I witnessed the care, concern, and outright selfless way in which they loved on their own children, and quite frankly, others around them. I learned a lot just by watching them, but I can't help but wonder if I would have become an even greater mom to my girls had we not moved away. It wasn't just about watching them, it was also having their physical support and encouragement as well, something I didn't have from my own mother while raising my girls. I understand that raising children is not an easy feat by any means and children aren't born with manuals that you can read and study to make sure you get everything right! I have often, and still do, feel very inadequate as a mother.

Like probably many of you, I suffer with imposter syndrome - thinking that I am just a mere fraction of the mother I would like to have been and often feel like a failure. I'm sure that many of these emotions stem from not having a mother-daughter relationship with my own mother. I often look at the friends that I have who are great mothers. Most of them have great mothers. I have deduced that great mothers beget great mothers and not-so-great mothers beget not-so-great mothers! Therefore, I have sealed my own fate! However, I do know that this is not necessarily true! I do know that we are all capable of overcoming our histories and changing the trajectory of bad situations. I do know that God can help us create that which we have not experienced ourselves.

If you are like me and have had thoughts of inadequacy around parenting, just know that if you have taken it upon yourself to break the cycles and chains that have been pronounced on you from others, then you have already won, and you're probably a better parent than you think you are! I'm sure, like me, you haven't been perfect, but you have been better, and acknowledging, admitting, and overcoming all the statistics and obstacles, is half the battle!

There was a distinct time in my parenting that I felt negatively impacted my kids the most and that was when we moved to Birmingham, Alabama. Our journey from Rochester ended a year after The Dude graduated seminary when he was unable to find a church to pastor. Many churches were looking for someone older and more experienced, despite loving The Dude's preaching and teaching abilities. We moved back to Philadelphia in 1996, and he went back to work at the Philadelphia District Attorney's Office. He also became an associate minister at St. Matthew's Baptist Church in Williamstown, New Jersey under the leadership of Rev. Dr. Raymond M. Gordon, Sr. and First Lady Diane Gordon, who were both former members of our old church, 19th Street Baptist Church. The time we both spent at SMBC was God-ordained. We both learned so much there - lessons we would later put to great use as God called us to the pastorate ministry.

In August of 1998, God called The Dude to pastor Memorial Baptist Church in Buffalo, New York, so we were once again heading back to the cold, wintery abyss that is Upstate New York. Oh, how I hated the cold weather, but I was willing to go wherever God planned for us to go, partly out of naivete and partly out of fear of God!

I will readily admit that I hated Buffalo! Everyone who knows me knows that I hated Buffalo. I couldn't get past the weather, and I just couldn't see any real opportunities for growth there, but we had an assignment to complete, and it wasn't going to be because of me that we did not complete it! The best thing about Buffalo was that I didn't feel completely alone. Being a pastor's wife can be a very lonely and isolating journey. I talk about my experience in greater detail in my book, "First Lady: The Real Truth." Buffalo was a little more tolerable since our friends from Philly, Troy and Jill, and their two kids, Jordyn and Nia, were also in Buffalo where Troy pastored Calvary Baptist Church. Troy and Jill were also Eboni's godparents, so being able to have our girls grow up together was a special blessing. It was nice to have play dates for the girls and bring both families together for fellowship.

One of the things we promised to do as a family was to have family night with the girls each Friday evening or Saturday afternoon. We wanted to do something together so that the girls could feel a sense of stability, especially since this was technically our third relocation, and we didn't have family nearby. We didn't have a lot of money to do grand vacations like Disney World or beach trips, but we were close enough to Niagara Falls to do day trips or find something fun to do near the waterfront in Buffalo. Unfortunately, our biggest trips were often just traveling back to Philly for holidays.

Memorial Baptist Church was a very small church with a big heart. The people were nice enough, but we just couldn't see staying in Buffalo as a viable option for our family. We began talking about looking for another church somewhere else. We had no idea where to look. By this time, I was working at a law firm, and I began scouring the internet for leads. I stumbled across an ad for a Senior Pastor for

16th Street Baptist Church in Birmingham, Alabama on a Christian job posting site. I admit I wasn't super knowledgeable about the church, other than the bombing that took place there in 1963, and I certainly didn't think of Alabama as a feasible relocation for the Price family. We were northerners with no real interest in going to the south to live, but I gathered The Dude's resume and curriculum vitae together and submitted his name to the Pulpit Committee. Oh, and then I told him about it!

"I put your name in for a church in Alabama! Neither one of us have ever been, so maybe we will at least get to visit," I proclaimed.

Of course, he just looked at me in his usual, "What did you do?" glare and dismissed it. We didn't really think anything of it nor thought it would materialize into anything. I was certain that there would be a million applicants with much more experience trying to get that historic church. I was really surprised when out of over 300 applicants, The Dude had made the final cut of three. He was invited to preach at the church and interview with both the congregation and Pulpit Committee. The Pulpit Committee also came to Buffalo to see him in a worship setting at Memorial. I won't go into all the details, but before we knew it, he was offered the position of pastor, accepted it in November 2001, and he was in the pulpit on the 1st Sunday in January 2002 as the newly elected Senior Pastor of the historic 16th Street Baptist Church of Birmingham, Alabama!

Why did I say that this move affected my parenting negatively? Moving to Birmingham was indeed a culture shock, but it was also a greater responsibility than I think we realized. While we were adamant and intentional about spending family time together in Buffalo, it didn't quite materialize the way we wanted when we moved to Birmingham. The Dude's responsibilities were very demanding, often leaving us with very little time for family time. We also had to figure out this new southern living and get into a routine.

We had moved in the middle of the school year and the girls were uprooted and planted in a new school away from their friends and forced to adjust. I was also enrolled in college in Buffalo and I had to figure out how to continue my studies. It was just a LOT. Eventually the new lifestyle landed us in four separate corners, each trying to navigate our new normal and finding out how we fit in this new place, and that is what I regret the most.

I really feel that while Birmingham has been a great place to raise our girls, and has had its charms, we didn't really know how to make the transition smoother so that our family unit could have stayed in tact like it was in Buffalo. I know that I personally struggled with the change and didn't really have the skills or knowledge to be the parent that I wanted to be during that period in our lives.

  Unfortunately, when you have had trauma in your upbringing and have experienced unstable conditions in your life, it is not uncommon to repeat some of the generational patterns while parenting your own children. It would be years later before I realized that I had done my girls a disservice in areas of my parenting, specifically during the early years of our move that we never quite recovered from. I was far removed from the shining examples and encouragements of a Momma Ford or a Doddie Franklin. I was carrying the responsibilities of being a pastor's wife for a well-known church and providing support to him, being a mom raising her children without any help or guidance and being a full-time student trying to better myself and find my way in the world. Again, it was a LOT!

  I am, however, grateful that I have been able to discuss these subjects with my girls openly and honestly and ask for their forgiveness for any harm my lack had caused them. We have been able to approach healing together, something that has not happened between my own mother and me. I was and am determined to stop the cycle of mother-hurt so that if my girls decide to ever become mothers, they will be so through a place of wholeness and healing and not the brokenness through which I mothered them. Even if mothering is not their desire or reality, they will know that their mother loves them unconditionally and is committed to showing them and supporting them despite her own frailties.

Eboni Paige and Amyna Janel, you are the air that I breathe - my heart in human form. You are gifts I don't deserve but am forever grateful for. I am extremely proud of both of you and the gems you are to this world. Continue to be a force in this universe and let them know you were here! Despite me, you are! Love you to life!

-Mom

WORD GIRLZ

"The Lord is my strength and my shield; in him my heart trusts, and I am helped; my heart exults, and with my song I give thanks to him." -Psalm 28:7

Being a mother is one of the most profound and challenging roles anyone can undertake. For those who didn't have a good mother as a role model, this task can feel even more daunting. The shadow of a difficult childhood may cast doubts and fears on your ability to parent well. But take heart—God's grace is sufficient, and His love is your guiding light.

You might worry about repeating the patterns of the past but remember that you are not bound by them. In Christ, you are a new creation. He redeems our past and equips us for the present. Lean into His love and let Him fill the gaps where your own mother fell short.

God understands our imperfections and does not expect us to be perfect parents. What He desires is our willingness to seek Him, to lean on His wisdom, and to allow His love to flow through us to our children. When you feel overwhelmed, remember that you don't have to do this alone. The Lord is your strength and your shield. He will help you, guide you, and provide you with the wisdom you need.

Parenting God's way means walking in love, patience, and grace. It means asking for forgiveness when you make mistakes and extending the same forgiveness to your children. It's about creating an environment where love and faith can flourish. When you parent from a place of God's love, you are planting seeds that will grow into the hearts of your children.

So, dear mother, be encouraged. You are not defined by your past, but by the love of Christ that surrounds you now. Take each day as it comes, lean into God's promises, and trust that He will help you thrive in this beautiful calling. Your journey as a mother is unique, and with God by your side, you will nurture your children with a love that reflects His own.

Let your heart exult in the Lord, knowing that His strength is made perfect in your weakness. Give thanks for the opportunity to mother in His grace, and trust that as you seek to parent God's way, He will provide all that you need.

Prayer: Heavenly Father, thank You for Your unfailing love and grace. Help me to lean into Your strength and wisdom as I mother my children. Fill the gaps left by my own upbringing with Your perfect love. Guide me to parent in a way that honors You and help me to trust in Your promise that You are with me every step of the way. In

Jesus' name, Amen.

Eboni Paige Price came into the world in Philadelphia, PA at 5:25 pm on Tuesday, May 5th, 1992, exactly two weeks to the date of our 2nd wedding anniversary. The pregnancy was perfect and although she played peek-a-boo at delivery, she arrived safe and sound, and very alert from the beginning. We had picked out a few names: Alyssa, Eboni and Amber, and others I can't remember, but the day she was born there was something about her that screamed Eboni with an "i," lol. Ebony, one of the most exotic, rare, and expensive woods is a dark wood native to west Africa and just a few other places. Eboni is definitely all of those - exotic, rare, EXPENSIVE and VERY afrocentric, lol. But she has always brought us nothing but pure joy.

Amyna Janel Price was born in Rochester, NY on Sunday, December 11, 1994 at 12:35 am. Her name means Amen and we knew that she was the final stamp on our family. From the very beginning she was super observant. Unlike her sister, who would go to anyone, Amyna didn't play that! lol She was very picky about who she allowed to hold her, and she is still that way with protecting her space. She literally taught herself how to write her name and we knew then that she would be a force in this world! We praise God for our rainbow baby and how she continually impacts our lives and those around her.

III. HEALING

CHAPTER 7: Forgiveness is the Road Less Traveled

"Forgiveness is not always easy. At times, it feels more painful than the wound we suffered, to forgive the one that inflicted it. And yet, there is no peace without forgiveness."
-Marianne Williamson

"When was the last time you talked to your mother?" I recall Arthur saying one day. Honestly, it took me a while to recall the last time. That was the reality of our relationship. We just didn't really talk. We checked on one another occasionally, but outside of that, there was no real connection or purposeful communication. After he said that I tried to be more intentional about calling her, but, honestly, it was not natural for me to do so. I had lived all my adulthood, after the age of eighteen, without a steady presence of her in my life. I did not call my mother when something exciting happened in my life. I did not call my mother when challenging things happened in my life. I did not seek her advice or approval about anything. I called merely to make sure she was okay; that was the only reason, and as you can see, sometimes I had to be reminded to do that. Don't misunderstand me, I didn't have any ill feelings or malice against her, it just wasn't a normal mother-daughter relationship. I was beyond the years of needing mothering, and we hadn't really built up a relationship that would allow for us to be friends in my adulthood. I made a point to go visit her whenever we went to Philly, but I found myself unable to stay longer than about thirty minutes or so. It was just awkward to me; I can't really explain it. I did make sure she spent time with the girls and allowed them to stay the night for a few days so that she could have a relationship with them.

 Even with everything I have gone through with my mother, I was never angry with her or desired to walk away from her, but there was a point when I realized that I needed to forgive her. I recall hearing God's prompting to forgive her when we lived in Rochester. I was on the phone with her one day and somehow something that happened during my childhood came up, which was a very rare occasion, and instead of her acknowledging it, addressing it, or even taking accountability, her reply was, "Well, you turned out okay, anyway!" It was the most hurtful thing she could have said to me. She has never acknowledged the impact her poor choices have had on my life. However, after I got off the phone, I felt the Lord gently whisper, "You need to forgive her." I asked Him how I could possibly do that; especially given the attitude she had just shown. Then, I remember sitting down and feeling as if the Lord was guiding me through my mother's life, moment by moment. I recalled everything I knew she had endured and the circumstances that shaped her. In that moment, my heart softened. I became empathetic, non-judgmental, and understanding, and that set me on the path to forgiving my mother.

I said that it led me on the path toward forgiveness, I didn't forgive overnight. I came to realize much later in my life that I still had more internal work to do to fully embrace that forgiveness. It's easy to say you've forgiven someone when you don't talk to them or see them often.

There were times when I would occasionally pay her way to come visit us - whether it was while we lived in Rochester, Buffalo, or Birmingham, I did invite her to spend a few days here and there with us. I mostly wanted her to have a relationship with her grandkids if nothing else.

One particular time she visited our home in Birmingham, she came with her brother's daughter, LaSherrie, whom she had taken in from the age of two when her parents could not care for her. It baffled me why she would take in someone else's child, when she wasn't really the mothering type. Honestly, I felt that she either did it for the stipend she received for her, or she was trying to do a "do over" of sorts in the mothering department. It amazed me that she did a lot of things with LaSherrie that she didn't do when I was growing up. Now, don't get me wrong, I wasn't jealous, just observant. She took a lot of interest in LaSherrie's school and her continual involvement in the Parent Association got her a small job at the school. When she and LaSherrie came to visit, I was a student at the University of Alabama at Birmingham. I was also in the Honors Program and had to go to the school one evening for an event, so I took my mother, LaSherrie, and my girls along. While we were driving along, my mother began to tell me that she was legally adopting LaSherrie.

"She's going to be your sister!" she said.

"No, she won't be my sister. She's my cousin," I replied. She then kept saying it more emphatically and she began to laugh about it. "No, she'll be your sister, and the adoption will be finalized on your birthday! November 3rd!"

I couldn't believe what I was hearing! Was this lady serious? I didn't care that she was adopting LaSherrie. Good for her! Her parents were not very involved in her life, so if my mother stepped in so she could have someone, then good for her! But how dare you laugh at the fact that you are adopting her on MY birthday? Why was that funny? How do you think I should reply to this? What did I ever do to her to make her feel like it was okay to tell me that she was basically replacing me on my birthday? Why did she have to even tell me that the adoption would be final on that day? What made matters worse is that she tried to get my daughter, Eboni, to laugh with her at MY expense! I was so furious that I pulled the car over, unlocked the door, and asked her if she knew where she was and how to get back home? She laughed it off, but I was very serious! When we got back into the house, I pulled my daughter into the back room.

"You know that grandmom and I have a strained relationship, right? You know that I didn't have a great relationship with her coming up, right?" I said to which she replied, "Yes."

"Well, what she did to me this evening was very insensitive. It made me feel horrible. But I don't ever want you to let anyone, ANYONE, get you to help them treat someone like she treated me this evening. You are never to make people feel like she made me feel and I don't care who it is. You do not participate. Do you understand?" Eboni said, "Yes. I'm sorry, mom." I hugged her and told her it was okay and not her fault. That was the last time my mother came to visit us in Birmingham (outside of my college graduation). I won't even go into detail about how her relationship with LaSherrie ended because it's not my story to tell, but let's just say it didn't end well at all.

The real test of true forgiveness came when my mother moved in with us in 2019. Let's be clear, I asked her to move in with us. I had hoped that it would be the beginning of us turning our relationship around.

The first year my mother lived with us was quite good. The year before, I had joined Teach for America (TFA) as an English teacher, fulfilling a lifelong dream. When I was a teenager watching my cousins during the summer, I would give them classwork to keep them occupied and help them retain information. Somehow, I instinctively knew how important that was.

In my senior year of high school, I dreamed of going to Morris Brown College in Atlanta or Mary McLeod Bethune Cookman College in Florida for Early Childhood Education. However, when it was time to fill out those applications, I felt disillusioned. My mother was in the beginning stages of her addiction, and all I could see were obstacles. There was no money to send me to school, and I worried about what would happen if her addiction worsened while I was away. Who would help me? With so many dilemmas swirling in my mind, I didn't know how to overcome them. My dream of being a teacher was delayed.

When I went to college as an adult (I got three degrees after the age of thirty), I fell in love with communications, specifically public relations, and graduated in 2006. However, I couldn't get a job in the public relations field in Birmingham which led me on the path of writing and publishing a few books, e-books, and creating my own national lifestyle magazine, WOW! Magazine, for Christian women.

In 2012, I finally landed a job at the Jimmie Hale Mission. I was initially hired as a Development Specialist, and eventually promoted to a public relations position where I could fully utilize my education and skills. I would eventually go on to start my own public relations business, helping entrepreneurs and business owners with strategy and branding.

In 2018, I saw an ad for TFA and felt it was the perfect time to pursue my dream of becoming a teacher. I was accepted into the 2018 Corps in Alabama and began my journey into education. My first year, I taught ninth and tenth grade English at Woodlawn High School in

Birmingham. The following year, the year my mother moved in with us, I taught seventh grade at Bush Hills STEAM Academy.

Every day when I got off work from teaching, my mother greeted me in our upstairs den. She ate her meals upstairs and she watched television with The Dude and me on most evenings until she retired to her room, located in the lower level of our home. She also attended church with us on Sundays and joined us when we went out to eat after church each Sunday.

As I mentioned, that first year was wonderful. Soon after, we were all thrust into a global pandemic that lasted for the next three years. During that time, I'm not entirely sure when, my mother started to retreat more and more into isolation. She stopped coming upstairs, and it became common for us not to see her during the week unless we happened to run into her downstairs. I definitely felt the divide between us deepen soon after June 28, 2021, when I discovered the true identity of my father. A few days later I mustered up the courage to ask my mother the questions I needed answers to about my father and what I had discovered.

I began the conversation by assuring her that I was not judging her, I simply wanted honest answers to my questions.

"Do you remember when I was around twelve and you introduced me to Anthony Mitchell and told me he was my father?" I asked.

"Yes," she replied.

"And do you remember when we went to live with Bobbie, and one day Terry Mitchell came to the house, and you told me he was my father?"

"Yes," she answered again.

"So, who do you believe is my father?"

"Anthony," she said without hesitation.

"Why?" I asked, seeking clarity.

"Because I was with him the longest," she explained, sharing a little bit about their relationship and why she thought he was my father.

I then told her, "Well, I just found out through Ancestry.com that Terry is, in fact, my father." Her expression was hard to read, a mix between an "oh, well" and a "hmmm."

I asked more questions, hoping to finally get the answers I had been seeking for nearly fifty-six years. Instead, I walked away with even more questions and quite annoyed. I felt she wasn't forthright about many things, and for others, she simply said she couldn't remember. When I expressed that I just wanted to know about my father, she shifted the conversation to her own struggles with her father's presence in her life, despite him always being around but not in the way she wanted. Once again, I felt unheard and invisible.

To make matters worse, I overheard her laughing about the situation on the telephone to someone. "Neither one of them did anything for her," I heard her say. "She had her heavenly father," then she laughed.

This not only hurt my feelings deeply but also marked the beginning of a serious breakdown in our relationship.

Dear reader, I wish I could share a story with a beautifully resolved ending, where my mother and I overcame our many obstacles and emerged triumphant. Unfortunately, that is not our reality. The past few years have been challenging, filled with triggers, strain, and moments that felt unbearable. I've had to lean heavily on serious prayer and therapy to maintain a healthy spiritual and psychological mindset, allowing me to continue thriving in the purpose God has ordained for my life.

It is not easy to forgive someone who continues to break trust and disregard your feelings, especially when they reside in the same house, but God continues to be faithful in His lovingkindness toward me and I am grateful for the love and support from my family and closest friends.

Therapy taught me what forgiveness truly is and what it is not. Forgiveness does not mean forgetting or condoning the wrongdoing or reconciling a relationship (sometimes reconciliation is not possible). You can forgive someone without believing that their actions were acceptable or justified. Forgiveness is a decision to overcome the pain inflicted by another person. It involves letting go of anger, resentment, shame, and other emotions associated with the injustice, even when those feelings are entirely reasonable. Forgiveness means treating the offender with compassion, even if they don't deserve it.

Once I embraced these truths, processed my pain and feelings toward my mother, and empathized with her own life journey, I was able to come to a place of forgiveness with her. After many more infractions over the last several years and her inability and refusal to change her behavior toward me, it became clear that reconciliation was not achievable. I pray for her mind, for her complete healing, and for deliverance from her personal pain. Despite everything, I am grateful that my husband and I can provide a place for her to reside in her later years.

WORD GIRLZ

"Be kind to one another, tenderhearted, forgiving one another, as God in Christ forgave you." - Ephesians 4:32

Forgiveness is one of the most profound acts of love we can extend to others, yet it is often one of the most challenging. When we are hurt, betrayed, or mistreated, our natural response is to hold onto that pain and let it shape our interactions. But as followers of Christ, we are called to a higher standard, one that reflects the forgiveness we have received from Him.

In the midst of His suffering on the cross, Jesus uttered words that exemplify the depth of His forgiveness: "Father, forgive them, for they know not what they do" (Luke 23:34). Despite enduring unimaginable pain and betrayal, Jesus chose forgiveness. His sacrifice on the cross was the ultimate act of love and mercy, offering us forgiveness for our sins and a restored relationship with God.

Forgiveness does not mean forgetting the wrongs done to us or excusing the behavior. It means choosing to release the hold that anger, resentment, and pain have on our hearts. Colossians 3:13 instructs us, "Bear with each other and forgive one another if any of you has a grievance against someone. Forgive as the Lord forgave you." When we remember how much we have been forgiven, it becomes easier to extend that same grace to others.

It's important to recognize that forgiveness and reconciliation are not always the same. While forgiveness is a personal act of letting go, reconciliation involves the restoration of a relationship, which may not always be possible or healthy. Romans 12:18 encourages us, "If it is possible, as far as it depends on you, live at peace with everyone." Sometimes, despite our best efforts, reconciliation may not occur. However, God can still be glorified in our lives through our obedience in forgiving others and striving to live in peace.

As we navigate the challenges of forgiveness, we must continually look to Christ, who has shown us the greatest love by forgiving us. His example teaches us to extend compassion and mercy, even when it is difficult. By doing so, we reflect His love to a world in desperate need of grace.

CHAPTER 8: The Antwon Fisher Effect

"In family life, love is the oil that eases friction, the cement that binds closer together, and the music that brings harmony."
-Friedrich Nietzsche

June 29, 2021, is a day I'll always cherish, as it felt like a second birth for me. Though I was born on November 3, 1966, and experienced a spiritual rebirth on October 2, 1977, June 29, 2021, marked my rebirth into a new family.

 Before I get into the details of that historic night, I need to clarify a little further my feelings toward the possible two-daddy situation.

 After Anthony Mitchell showed up out of the blue and

my mother declared him my father, I didn't see him again during my childhood. He would resurface when I was an adult, married, and the mother of two. Somehow my mother reconnected with him while The Dude and I were living in Rochester and when we moved back to Philly, he asked to take me out to dinner. I don't know the details of this reconnection between him and my mother, but it seemed like they were dating to me. During that dinner he brought out some artifacts of his life: his military experience, work he did under the Carter administration, things he was proud of, I suppose. I couldn't help but feel unimpressed. How was I supposed to react with this revelation that he was out here living his best life while I was fatherless? Especially since he came into my life for one night and then disappeared AGAIN. I tried to be upbeat and let bygones be bygones, but he never pursued a relationship with me after that. There I was feeling abandoned AGAIN. The only positive thing from it was the relationship I began to develop with his daughter, Bridgette, whom I believed was my little sister.

Bridgette Mitchell was about thirteen years old when Anthony introduced her to me. She was adorable and I instantly fell in love with her. I had always wanted a little sister, so she was perfect. When Arthur and I moved away to go to seminary, we lost touch and when Anthony came back into my life, Bridgette wasn't in Philadelphia, if I recall correctly. Years later we would reconnect because I purposely went looking for her. I had to find Anthony in order to find her (he and my mother were no longer acquainted, and he was married to another woman by this time). I tried my best to build a relationship with him, visiting him and his wife every time I visited Philadelphia, but he still couldn't manage to be a consistent presence in my life (which I would discover he couldn't do with any of his children).

Despite the lack of relationship with Anthony, Bridgette and I would go on to build a wonderful and very close sisterhood. We shared the middle name Antoinette, we looked alike, and we had similar likes and personalities. To this day we try to get together at least once a year. In the back of my mind, I always had questions about these two men. Bridgette was really the reason why I was convinced that Anthony was my father. You couldn't tell us we weren't sisters! We were both fascinated by the similarities between us.

The revelation I made through ancestry.com that Tyrone Machio Palmer Mitchell, aka Terry, was my biological father, was a complete shocker to my entire being. This revelation came to light because his brother, Brian Mitchell, appeared as my top DNA match on the platform. To delve deeper into this incredible discovery, I reached out to Brian's daughter, Atiya, through ancestry and Facebook. Our conversation started like this:

> *Hi Atiya! hope you're doing well. I saw your family tree on ancestry and believe we are related - I'm trying to see if I'm connected to Evangeline (Palmer) Mitchell and specifically her son, Tyrone (Terry) Mitchell. I see connections between your tree and others that I have found a DNA match to.*

> *Wow!!! When I saw your picture, I thought you looked like Malaika. That's Terry's daughter. Interesting. Well, if you want to talk to the family, we're having our monthly Powwow on Zoom this Saturday. Call me.*

I called Atiya, and she was eager to connect me with Terry's daughter, Malaika, and his son, Terrell, via Facebook Messenger video chat. The conversation with Terrell is one I'll never forget. "Hi, how are you? What's your name?," he said.

"My name is Corawana, though it says Candie on Facebook."

"Oh, ok," as if the name specification was validation for him. "I know who you are. You're my sister, Corawana. Daddy always told us who you were."

I was flabbergasted! "Wait. What do you mean, you know who I am?"

"Daddy always told us we had a sister. Corawana." He

then went on to talk about Terry a little. Terry had passed in 2000, yet it was clear to me just from this conversation that Terrell never recovered from his death. I would go on to talk to most of my siblings and find this true for each of them.

Later that day I connected with Malaika through Facebook messenger:

Hi, Malaika. It's nice to meet you.

Good morning. It's a pleasure to meet you, too. Our father made sure to tell us about you while growing up."

Oh wow!!!! I would not have imagined that - that makes me happy.

Absolutely, we have always known your name and that you were our eldest sister.

That's crazy!! I just put all of these pieces together yesterday! The connection to who I was related to on ancestry! It's a bit overwhelming... but not in a bad way.

Malaika then went down the line of Terry's children, my siblings, and where everyone was, to her knowledge. We continued to connect through video chats and texts.

Later that same day, Atiya added me to the family WhatsApp chat, and from that moment on, my phone was flooded with messages of welcome and love. For the rest of the day and well into the next, heartfelt messages poured in, inviting me into the family with open arms. This is why I call this chapter "The Antwon Fisher Effect." In the 2002 movie Antwon Fisher, starring Derek Luke and Denzel Washington, Antwon discovers his paternity and meets his father's family. Near the end, he is welcomed into his paternal grandmother's house, where the entire family greets him with a feast fit for a king. I remember watching that movie and being deeply moved by the love and acceptance he finally received after enduring so much hardship. Every child deserves that kind of acceptance and love. I cried during that scene and now, here I was, having my own Antwon Fisher experience. For two whole days, my family welcomed me, making me feel like I truly belonged.

Saying I was overwhelmed would be an understatement. I was trying desperately to process all the information I received in just a short time. First, I couldn't quite wrap my mind around the fact that two of Terry's children said they had known about me their entire lives, that Terry made sure they knew I was their oldest sister. What did that mean? How did those conversations come about? The writer in me imagined a wonderful, heartwarming story of a father who kept his daughter's name. The broken child in me just had more questions, more angst, and more sadness because I will never actually know.

Second, I now had this entire family, complete with

uncles, aunties, and cousins who not only acknowledged me as their kin but accepted me as well. While my grandmother, Evangeline, and her husband, John Mitchell, were no longer with us, all my father's siblings were still alive! I was so grateful to meet Raina, Brian, Vernere, Johnny, Carlton, Vanessa, and their families.

Though I was scared, I felt deeply thankful. I had heard stories from friends who, upon discovering a paternity secret, were met with anything but open arms. I couldn't help but wonder if this interest in me would last or if I would eventually face the same rejection I had experienced with other family members. For now, though, I chose to embrace the warmth and acceptance they offered, hoping it would endure.

On July 3, 2021, I joined the Mitchell family for their monthly Zoom call, and my mind was completely blown. As soon as I joined, my cousin, Atiya, greeted me warmly and began sharing her screen, which was filled with photos from the family album. She took special care to point out who everyone was in the photos, especially my father, Terry. I had never seen any of those pictures before, and I was captivated.

After showing the photos, Atiya mentioned that she would be sharing some documents found among my grandmother Evangeline Mitchell's effects in the family home. Evangeline was known for documenting everything, and these documents served as historical artifacts for the family. Among them were pages dedicated to each of her children and their families. Atiya started with the first document, a page dedicated to her firstborn, my father, Tyrone Machio Palmer Mitchell. It included his name, birth and death dates, paternity, marriage information, and a list of his eight children. The order of children was listed as follows: Alphonso, Tyrone Jr., Corawana Tribble, Azzizez, Yadillia, Malaika, Tahira, and Terrell.

Seeing my name on that page left me completely stunned. I interrupted Atiya and asked, "Wait. Wait a minute. Who wrote this?" Someone replied, "Mom (Evangeline). That's her handwriting." I was so overwhelmed that I had to step off camera for a moment to process everything. My grandmother, Evangeline Mitchell, knew about me! I realized that in the past few days of getting to know this family, I had never told any of them my maiden name, yet here it was on a family document! Terry had told his mother and children about my existence. (Parenthetically, let me tell you that his mother not only knew about me, but she also made sure my name -though misspelled - was included as one of his children on his obituary!) Even so, none of his siblings knew about me.

Atiya then asked me to address the family and share

how I found them, giving me the opportunity to revisit the extent of my exposure to Terry, which I relayed to them.

I first met Terry when he unexpectedly showed up at my great-grandmother's house. This was back in the days of landline phones, there were no cell phones and beepers were just on the horizon, but not yet popular. How did he find his way there that day? I have no idea! When I asked my mother, she said she couldn't remember.

"These two men, both potential fathers for the daughter you've been raising without them, show up out of the blue, and you don't remember either of the conversations you had with them?" I asked incredulously.

"No, I don't remember," she replied.

I wanted to know what explanations they gave for not being in my life. I wanted to know what they intended to do after that day. Did she hold them accountable? Did she demand that they do better? Did they promise to do better? Why were they there? And even more importantly, why did they leave again???

I can't understand how she doesn't remember the day her daughter's potential fathers showed up out of the blue, but that's her story, and she's sticking to it.

She gave me nothing, just like she had done my whole life. Terry isn't around to fill me in and Anthony decided not to reply to my inquiry. Go figure.

On that unexpected visit, Terry took me on a motorcycle ride, and I saw him at least two more times. The second time, he introduced me to Terry Jr. and Azziz, affectionately called "Zee." "These are your brothers, " he said. I remembered that Terry Jr. was older, and Zee was younger, placing me right in the middle in terms of age. Terry took us to see The Wiz at the movies, which Zee later confirmed in a conversation when we reconnected.

"I remember you, sis! Every time I see the movie, The Wiz, I think of you. I made sure my kids watched it and I would say, 'I went to see that with my sister! I remember when daddy picked you up and we were going to the movies. He asked you what you wanted to see, and you said, 'The Wiz.' I was so irritated! I wanted to see something else. But I loved it and was skipping out the movie theatre to Ease on Down the Road! I never forgot that because I would have never seen a movie like that otherwise."

I had honestly forgotten about it, but it was good to hear him say that watching the movie gave him fond memories of me!

The third and last time I saw Terry, he invited me to meet him at a house in North Philadelphia. I later discovered that it was the family home, where he and all his siblings were raised. His brother, Carlton, still lives there to this day.

Not wanting to go alone, I asked my god sister, Sharron

Brown, to come with me since it was close to her house, literally just a few blocks away. My memory of that evening is mostly a blur, except for a few small details. I recall a woman being there, though her face escapes me. I remember Terry showing us a photo album, and Sharron saying, "Who is this? She looks just like you!" I believe Terry responded that it was his sister.

I later asked Sharron if she could remember any details I had forgotten. She confirmed that we had indeed visited the home and that there was a woman there. She sensed that the woman was a little unfriendly. Sharron also remembered the photo album and her declaration that I resembled one of his siblings. Unfortunately, that's all she could remember as well and that was the last time I saw Terry Mitchell.

When I mentioned this memory to the family on the Zoom call, my Aunt Vanessa asked how old I was when I visited the house. I told her I was around 14 or 15. She vaguely remembered Terry bringing a teenage girl to the house one day and saying, "This is my daughter." She said she shrugged it off and didn't take him seriously.

Terry had a huge personality, and they didn't always know when to believe him. Like the time he told them he helped train Venus and Serena Williams (he was a tennis professional)—of course, they didn't believe him, yet there was a condolence card sent by one of them which was read at his funeral. I laughed when I heard that. I wish I had known him.

That Zoom call left me spinning with emotions. I moved from awe to sadness, then gratefulness, and back to sadness again in the span of minutes. It was a lot to process, but I'm thankful that The Dude, my girls, my therapist, and my closest friends were there to help me navigate through all of my emotions.

At fifty-four years old, most of us believe we've already found our lifelong friends—the ones life has shown us are our true support system. Yet, there I was, about to discover a whole new village I never knew existed, and not only is it a large one, but we share DNA! My mother's side of the family is small, so encountering this expansive new family felt like managing many moving parts. I decided to take it one family unit at a time, but I was determined to connect with anyone who wanted to get to know me because I wholeheartedly wanted to get to know them.

Spread across Philly, New Jersey, Atlanta, Virginia, and Charlotte, my newfound family prompted me to embark on a family tour to meet and build relationships with as many of them as possible. Uncle Brian and his wife, Angilee, lived just two hours away in Atlanta and I visited them monthly for a while! I made annual trips to Philly/New Jersey and Charlotte and spent a week in Virginia getting to know two of my sisters.

   Meeting my family brought me a profound sense of completion. When you're unsure of your origins or missing a piece of your identity, it leaves you feeling incomplete, with more questions than answers. Despite the fact that I never had the chance to know my father, his family has given me a cherished sense of belonging. Through countless conversations, they've made me feel seen and understood in ways I never experienced growing up. What continually amazed all of us are the striking resemblances I and my children have with members of the family. I believe that the picture my god sister noticed at the house visit was my Aunt Vernere. If you put a picture of the two of us side by side in the 1980s, you will be hard pressed to determine who is who. My daughter, Eboni, and I both resemble my sister, Malaika, and a younger picture of my daughter, Amyna, looks exactly like a younger Terry. I even resemble Terry's first cousin, Sandra, more than her own daughter!

   It's amazing how God ensured I wouldn't leave this earth without knowing my roots. His love for me is evident in how this journey has deepened my gratitude and enriched the relationships and ministry He entrusted me with.

   Feeling loved enables you to love better, and feeling seen allows you to see others more clearly. I can't adequately express my gratitude for their presence in my life—they've shown me immense grace and understanding, cheered me on at crucial moments, given me shoulders to cry on, and embraced my family wholeheartedly.

One of the ways I chose to honor my entry into the Mitchell family was by taking on my father's last name. While the Tribble name represented my ancestry through my mother's side and her father's lineage, I never had the opportunity to carry my father's surname.

I have never seen an actual copy of my birth certificate (I had to send for a copy when I was getting married), so I didn't know if there was a father's name listed on the original or not. During the process of getting my passport, I had to obtain a long form of my original birth certificate which meant I had to contact the Vital Records in Pennsylvania with a copy that showed more information such as parents, etc. Lo and behold when the copy came back, the father listed was Terry Mitchell! Not his entire legal name, which makes me think he didn't personally sign it, but nonetheless his name is listed! I was floored! I could have known for sure so many years ago and pursued confirmation! (Of course, I asked my mother about it and you guessed it, gentle reader, she doesn't remember anything!)

Making the decision to legally change my last name to

Mitchell-Price was a deeply personal journey—it allowed me to claim my story, embrace it fully, and establish my own legacy. It also strengthened my bond with my siblings who already bore the Mitchell name. I'm grateful that my entire family supported and understood this important step I needed to take for myself.

The only part of this story that pulled my absolute heartstrings the most was informing Bridgette that I was not Anthony Mitchell's daughter, and therefore, not her biological sister. It was one of the hardest phone calls I have ever had to make. Bridgette had taken a DNA test through 23andme and I decided to take one on that platform as well so that we would know for sure if there was any biological relationship between the two of us, since both potential fathers had the same last name, and results turned out that there was no DNA shared between us. How God managed to meld two humans together as sisters so perfectly, only He knows. Despite biology, Bridgette will always be my sister, and I'm grateful that even through these crazy circumstances, He chose to make us sisters. He knew we would need each other, and no one will be able to stand between the bond we share.

WORD GIRLZ

"For I know the plans I have for you, declares the Lord, plans for welfare and not for evil, to give you a future and a hope." Jeremiah 29:11

In our journey through life, we are continually reminded of God's unwavering love for us. His love transcends time and circumstance, manifesting in countless ways to assure us of His presence and care.

God's intervention in our lives is purposeful and intentional. He orchestrates events and circumstances to align with His divine plan for each of us. Even in times of uncertainty, God's hand guides us towards our destined purpose in Christ.

Psalm 46:1 reminds us, "God is our refuge and strength, a very present help in trouble." Through life's storms and challenges, God's grace sustains us. His love provides us with strength, peace, and comfort, enabling us to weather every trial that comes our way. His grace is not just a concept but a tangible presence that carries us through our darkest moments.

God's love is often revealed through the people He places in our lives. Whether through family, friends, or mentors, God uses these relationships to demonstrate His love and encouragement. Proverbs 27:17 tells us, "As iron sharpens iron, so one person sharpens another." Each interaction and connection is a reminder of God's love working through others to uplift and support us on our journey.

Romans 8:28 assures us, "And we know that in all things God works for the good of those who love him, who have been called according to his purpose." Every experience, every relationship, every trial—God weaves them together to fulfill His purpose in our lives. He aligns our steps with His divine plan, leading us closer to our destiny in Christ.

May we rest in His promises, knowing that He is faithful to guide us and fulfill His purpose in our lives. Let us open our hearts to receive His love and extend it to others, bearing witness to His goodness and grace in all we do.

The family Zoom that started it all for me! July 3, 2021.

l - Maryamm Malaika Mitchell, my sister with our father, Terry.
. r- Eboni Paige Price, my daughter.

l - My father, Terry. r - Amyna Paige Price, my daughter. She used to say that she didn't look like me nor her father. She was out here looking like her grandfather!

Meanwhile, I was in the 80's looking like my Aunt Vernere (l)..

CHAPTER 9: Funeralizing Lost Relationships

"Take the time to grieve what you wish it was, and then accept what it actually is."
-Unknown

The past few years, I have been dedicated to healing from old wounds. Childhood trauma, often defined as a psychological response to deeply distressing events during one's early years, can have profound and lasting effects on adulthood. Trauma isn't always severe physical or mental abuse; it can also be subtle, like neglect, rejection, or a lack of loving support during crucial developmental years.

My journey toward healing began with forgiving my

mother, father, and other family members who, sometimes unknowingly, contributed to my feelings of neglect and invisibility. When I recognized that my mother was still engaging in behaviors that showed she didn't have my best interest at heart, I realized it was healthier for me to let go of the possibility of a relationship with her than to allow further harm. I had to mourn the relationship with my mother, the absence of my father, and any other toxic relationships in my life. This process, though painful, has been essential in my path to healing and finding peace.

One day recently the Lord placed in my spirit the following, which I wrote on my Facebook page:

God said, "Go ahead and mourn the relationships that have never materialized as you envisioned." Either He will change your expectation of it or keep it dead - but your healing will come when you accept it for what it is!

Later that day, I came across a video of a friend of mine, Dr. Sarita Lyons, speaking at a conference at which an attendee asked her the following question, "I wonder if you all have thoughts or wisdom for those who don't have strong relationships with their mother."

Dr. Sarita's response resonated with me so much that I had to include it in this book verbatim.

I don't ever think you grow out of needing your mom. Even people who have lost their mother, in terms of they're deceased, that's a deep, deep pain. But it's also painful to have your mother alive and feel like you don't have her. And for you to be full grown and there's like a baby in you, there's a little girl in you that still wants to be cared for and encouraged and affirmed, still needs attention. I want to affirm that that desire you have is good. You know when we read it, especially as a parent, we say, 'Yeah, honor your mother and father so that your days may be long upon the earth, that this is the only command given with a promise. Parents like to quote that for disobedient children, but it is true. There's a promise with that. But I think it's also important for us: what does that look like when you're an adult? What does it look like to honor your mother when sometimes they haven't even lived an honorable life? So, first thing I would say, in order for you to love your mom well and build a relationship with her and to honor her is to first grieve the loss of the mother you wish you had. And in some ways many of us have to have a homegoing celebration or we have to have a funeral in our own hearts and mind for the fantasy mom that I have to bury because she does not exist and that the pressure, the standard that I hold this woman to who is actually my mother, she may never get there. But what will it look like to have my deepest need satisfied in God, satisfied by other women that God will bring close to me? But I still thank God that this is the vessel He chose for me to come through. But I think grief, real grieving has to precede your ability to really love. Because sometimes we're loving a ghost and we're not loving the actual woman and who she really is. And I think grieving and allowing God to minister to you, to comfort you, and for you to see the resources of mothering He's surrounded you with, will help you meet her and actually, even though you're her child, you'll be able to minister to her in a way that you didn't think you'd be available to because of your pain."[1]

I wanted to come through my phone screen when I watched this video. I can't tell you how many times I replayed it, over and over again. I also in boxed Dr. Sarita to let her know that it was confirmation of what God had already told me.

Many people forget that not everyone has a wonderful, loving mother or a great relationship with her. Not every mother is affirming or supportive. Mother's Day and Father's Day are often filled with accolades for parents from their children, with countless social media posts dedicated to praising amazing parents. Unfortunately, not everyone can claim to have had the best parents. Dr. Sarita's advice makes perfect sense for anyone seeking to

---

1   Lyons, Sarita. Glory Livestream with Jackie Hill-Perry. October 27-28, 2023 https://www.facebook.com/share/r/HcYgtSHPdDL5o3Tj/?mibextid=Ls6BEq

heal from childhood trauma with either parent. Personally, I had to come to terms with the fact that I was holding onto a fantasy. There was a mother I longed for, believed I deserved, and hoped to have by bringing my mother to live with me, but she is not, nor is she choosing to be, that person. My mother is who she is, and I had to let go of the fantasy and mourn the relationship that didn't materialize to release the pain I had carried for so long. This realization extended to my father as well, as I confronted the feelings of loss and absence that plagued me. He is no longer with us, so I have to bury the relationship I was denied.

  I feel blessed that even though I had to mourn these relationships, God has given me other relationships that nurture the little girl within me. My aunts, uncles, and the special bonds I share with my cousins, have become a source of love and support, filling the void and helping me heal. God continually gives them the right words to say to me at the right times, the "just because" phone calls to check on me and my family, the invites to fellowship with them and be in their presence, or the safe places to land my thoughts and vents. It is all like gold to me; precious and valuable. I remain eternally grateful.

WORD GIRLZ

Whether your mother was a great mom or not so great, one undeniable truth stands: you are here! If you are reading this with any semblance of health and strength, it is because God's grace and mercy have sustained you despite whatever upbringing you experienced. God is Faithful!

For some, Mother's Day and Father's Day are filled with joy and gratitude for the wonderful parents they have. For others, these days can be a stark reminder of what was lacking—of the love, support, and nurturing that were missed. But take heart, dear reader, because no matter your experience with your mother, God's love for you has never wavered.

"Though my father and mother forsake me, the Lord will receive me." (Psalm 27:10, NIV)

God's love is steadfast and unchanging. You are always on His mind, and His plans for you are filled with hope and a future. Whether your mom is here or not, whether she was wonderful, absent, or hurtful, know that God used her as a vessel to bring you into this world so that His purpose and will could be manifested in you.

Whatever testimony you have about your mom—good, bad, or indifferent—it is a part of your story. And God can use every part of your story to bring healing and hope to others. Your experiences, even the painful ones, are not in vain. They are the threads that God weaves into a beautiful tapestry of grace and redemption.

"…in all things God works for the good of those who love him, who have been called according to his purpose." (Romans 8:28, NIV)

Trust in God to heal you from your childhood trauma. Allow Him to give you peace and the capacity to love despite how you grew up. His healing power is boundless, and His love can mend the deepest wounds.

"He heals the brokenhearted and binds up their wounds." (Psalm 147:3, NIV)

Embrace the truth that you are cherished by your Heavenly Father. Your life has meaning and purpose, and your story—every chapter of it—has the power to inspire and uplift others. Let God's love fill the gaps left by an imperfect childhood. Let His peace wash over you and renew your heart.

Know that you are a beloved child of God, perfectly created for His divine purposes. Trust Him, lean into His love, and watch how He transforms your past into a testimony of His faithfulness and grace.

CHAPTER 10: Stronger Didn't Kill Me

"As black women, we're always given these seemingly devastating experiences — experiences that could absolutely break us. But what the caterpillar calls the end of the world, the master calls the butterfly. What we do as black women is take the worst situations and create from that point."
-Viola Davis

Despite everything I've gone through, I can truly say that God has been a constant, present help throughout my journey! The enemy thought he would take me out from the very beginning, but God, indeed, had the last say! I still wrestle with some of the residue of my past, and I am grateful and thankful for every single struggle because it has not stopped the blessings God purposed for me to have.

When I tell you that growing up I had very low self-esteem, please believe me! I had shorter hair than everyone else, I didn't think I was pretty, and I didn't think I was smart. I was always inwardly comparing myself to others.

If there was nothing else I was adamant about doing when my girls were young, it was telling them that they were beautiful, and smart, and could do anything they put their minds to. I longed for that kind of validation growing up and I realize now how so important it is to validate not just our children, but any child that shares our space. I made this a daily practice in my role as a teacher - always validating my students, even to this day! Thankfully, those inner wars did not cause me to seek acceptance and love from the wrong places! I know that God had his hand all the way on my life! I have had guys who thought that if they said the right thing to me, I would crumble and let them have whatever they wanted. Too bad for them, I was not gullible nor naive! I had observed enough around me to know exactly where that kind of recklessness got you.

Church was my haven, and it probably was the main thing that kept me out of trouble. I know that it literally SAVED my life! I believe that because I seemingly made the right choices and had such a mild temperament, it caused people to see me as strong, properly aligned, and not in need of help. Dear reader, "STRONG" people aren't invincible! We need to stop thinking they can take anything just because they may not show vulnerability. At the end of the day, they are people with real feelings and challenges.

Despite being told I was stupid, I managed to go back to school and graduate magna cum laude and with honors with a Bachelors in Communications, specializing in Public Relations, and two master's degrees; one in Christian Education and one in Public Relations.

When I graduated from the University of Alabama at Birmingham in 2006, I couldn't find a job for six years, so during that time, I created my own job! I founded and edited WOW! Magazine, a national lifestyle magazine for Christian women that became extremely popular and successful. I taught myself how to create websites, I taught myself how to use top designer programs; and I had over 30 writers writing for me, most of whom I have never even laid eyes on face-to-face to this day! I have personally interviewed Sherri Shepherd, Donna Richardson (formerly Joyner), Joyce Meyer, Lois Evans, Mablean Ephraim, and more, and have had many celebrities grace our cover.

I managed to do all of this as a full-time wife and mother! I was determined to no longer listen to the internal doubts about my abilities. I eventually went on to publish two books, and became an entrepreneur, creating my own body butter line. I also checked off my bucket list my desire to be a teacher (a desire I had since my babysitting days with my little cousins) and taught seventh, ninth, and tenth grade English Language Arts in the Birmingham City School District.

I have been blessed to have so many amazing experiences alongside my husband and his position as Pastor of the Historic Sixteenth Street Baptist Church. We have met so many interesting people and celebrities from across the world, including having dinner with Oprah Winfrey, meeting the then Vice President, Joe Biden, John Lewis, Dalia Lama, Chris Tucker, Judge Ketanji Brown Jackson, and so many more!

Why is this all important? It's not me bragging! It's me being grateful because I want you to know that it is not about how you start. It is not about the irresponsible choices others have made for you. It is about how you choose to finish! Despite whatever it is, or whomever it is, that have caused trauma in your life, it is up to you to pivot, turn it around, and take possession of your own narrative!

When I think about all the things that could have happened to me in my life if I had decided to be a victim of my circumstances, it is frightening, but I refused to fall down and take it! The Lord knew that I would come to Him at an early age, that His Word would take root in my life even before I could fully grasp it because its job was to SAVE ME!!! He saw my marriage, He saw my kids, He saw my abilities, my gifts, my talents, all the way back in eternity and He knew that I was precious to Him. Even though I had to come through the two bloodlines I was assigned to, it would eventually be a testimony for the ages. In the midst of my bruises, He would make sure I survived and could bear witness of His glory so that I could help someone else!!!

There are a couple things I want to leave you with, if you get nothing else from my story:

1. Don't be so quick to try to process your trauma. Healing takes time.

I almost didn't move the needle toward healing. I had assumed that just because I had listened to God's voice when He told me to forgive my mother, and I began to be empathetic about her life, that I had forgiven her. I was quick to move on and not sit with my emotions, my feelings, and my pain. Healing doesn't happen overnight, nor does it happen just with a revelation. It takes time.

2. If you are silent about your pain, they will kill you and say you enjoyed it - Zora Neale Hurston

If I did not discover my paternity, I might not have been

faced with confronting my past. I had done such a good job of sucking it up and acting as if nothing had happened, that I would not have faced it head on. I probably would not have ever expressed my feelings to my mother. I had been voiceless all my life and was not accustomed to confronting and being honest about my feelings, especially to her.

3. GET A THERAPIST! Get help from a licensed professional to help you process your past, approach forgiveness the correct way, and move yourself toward healing!

4. Think on this: What is it like to be truly healed? When you're broken, all your relationships and everything you do exist through that brokenness. What would your relationships look like, what would be different in your life, if you were viewing them through healed eyes???

Brokenness has a way of muddying the waters of everything and everyone you touch! The scary thing is that you don't even realize that it is influencing your relationships, on how you interact with others, how you view yourself, how you walk in rooms, how others experience you! Yes, it can affect all those things which is why therapy can be so helpful. But what would your relationships look like if you were truly healed? Do yourself a favor and find out!

5. Check your most important relationship - your relationship with Christ! I know for a fact that I would not be in the right mind to even write this book, nor enjoy the life and love that I have, had it not been for my relationship with Jesus Christ! I would be even more of a mess without Him! If you've strayed away from His Word, His will, and His ways, GET BACK TO HIM! Experiencing God's love in your life, seeing things through the lens of the Word of God, and learning to trust Him despite what's happened to you, will revolutionize your life!

I realize that my story might not even seem particularly poignant to you, however, I do hope that you walk away knowing that even in the most broken of situations, there is healing, peace, and love available. You can walk straight outta brokenness. You can overcome all the icky, nasty things that have plagued your life for years, and you can be healed! I am a witness. I still have some issues and some turbulence. But I walked Straight Outta Brokenness, and it didn't kill me!!

WORD GIRLZ

Life's journey can be filled with unexpected turns and turbulent times that leave us feeling broken and weary. However, during our trials, we have a loving Savior who promises to order our steps and guide us through every storm.

Psalm 37:23 reassures us that our steps are ordered by the Lord. This means that even when life feels chaotic, God is in control, directing our paths with divine precision. We can find comfort in knowing that our lives are not left to chance; every step we take is part of His perfect plan.

Romans 8:28 reminds us that God works all things together for our good and His glory. Our challenges and hardships are not without purpose. God can turn our pain into a powerful testimony that can help and inspire others. When we trust in His ability to transform our circumstances, we open ourselves up to experiencing His joy and peace.

In Psalm 147:3, we see God as the healer of the brokenhearted. No matter how deep our wounds, God's love and grace are sufficient to heal and restore us. He promises to bind up our wounds, mending our brokenness with His tender care.

Proverbs 3:5-6 encourages us to trust in the Lord with all

our heart and not rely on our own understanding. When we submit to His will, He promises to make our paths straight. Trusting God means surrendering our fears, doubts, and plans to Him, believing that He knows what is best for us.

Are you facing a season of brokenness? Are you struggling to see how your current circumstances could possibly work out for your good? Take heart, dear friend. God's plans for you are filled with hope and a future (Jeremiah 29:11). He is the master at turning our messes into messages of hope and redemption.

Rejoice in the knowledge that brokenness will not kill you. God is with you, and He will deliver you if you put your trust in Him. Embrace the journey, knowing that every step is ordered by a loving and sovereign God who is working all things together for your good and His glory. Your story is not over; it is being beautifully rewritten by God Himself.

Candie and Oprah

"As the wife of the pastor of one of the most well-known churches in the world, I get to meet a lot of famous people. From having dinner with Oprah, meeting the Dalai Lama, to being known by John Lewis or discussing educational equity with Terrence Howard, it's been a very interesting journey! And, still, at the end of the day, fighting for kids to receive quality education, is still my most important experience."

As the Founder and Editor-in-Chief of WOW! (Women of the Word) Magazine, not only did I get to work with over 30 amazing writers from across the country, but I got to feature a plethora of people doing WOWderful things for Christ.

Dear Terry,

As I write this letter to you, I am lying in bed at your sister, Vernere's house in Charlotte, North Carolina. It is quite odd and exhilarating, to say the least. It is odd because before a year ago, I didn't know Aunt Vernere or any of your family. It is exhilarating because this time of getting to know your family has been filled with acceptance and love. I didn't get the opportunity to know you, but I feel somewhat connected to you through your family. It is indeed a paradox of sorts as I navigate the reality of not knowing you with knowing you through your siblings and your other children.

Your siblings still talk of you fondly, but they don't spare me from the parts of you that were flawed and human, which I totally appreciate.

I can clearly see the hold you still have on your children when they talk of you with an almost cultish longing. It's been twenty-two years since you left them, yet their pain still seems new and raw. However, you left me fifty-six years ago, so I can't relate to their experience of you, nor their incessant need to promulgate your presence, your words of wisdom, and your very essence into almost every conversation with me. My pain is also still new and raw, but for obviously different reasons.

You fathered eight children (four boys and four girls), yet as far as I can tell or have been told, five of them were given the opportunity to know you on some level, and three were not. I landed in the latter group. Born the first girl, and the third child, I have so many unanswered questions. Did you come to the hospital when I was born? Your name is on my birth certificate. Did you sign it? Did you experience the feelings that come over new dads when their newborns arrive, especially when they are girls? Were you proud? Were you happy? Did you feel a need to protect me from the evils of the world? If so… why didn't you?

As I reflect on the day I finally met you at approximately 13 years old, I am even more flabbergasted than ever. What were you thinking when you met me? I don't remember our conversation. Did you talk to me at all? I don't remember you asking about my interests, what I liked to do, how I was doing in school. How I was doing without you. There must have been something that pricked your heart, invaded your soul because I saw you again, at least twice. It must have been important for you to want me to go to your family's home. What were you thinking as you watched me sitting in your family's house looking at family photos? Did you hear my god sister say I looked like your sister? I now know that she was right! I was the spitting image of Aunt Vernere! Did you notice that, too? Looking at pictures of you and I as children I mirrored your face. Is that what convinced you that I was your daughter?

Did you want to be my father? How did it feel to see your first girl-child? Why was that the last time I saw you? Were you disappointed with me? Were you too busy to be bothered? Why was it important for you to tell your mother about me? What did you say to her? What was her response? Did she want to know me? Was the act of her putting my full legal name and birth order among your other children, her way of tucking me into her heart? Did she think about me? I was floored to know that she put me among your children on your obituary. She had no clue whether I was dead or alive, but it was important for her to include me. I wish I had known what you two talked about as it related to me. I would like to think that it was meaningful especially since it was also important for you to tell each of your kids that I existed. Did you try to find me?

I legally changed my last name to Mitchell-Price. It felt like the right thing to do. It is my birthright, and I felt like I needed to take ownership of my own story, to redeem somehow the time that is forever lost between us.

I have so many questions and will never get the answers. Sometimes I am angry with you. Other times I am grateful. Sometimes I am jealous of the way your kids talk about you. Other times I am grateful. My life wasn't easy. It

has been filled with a lot of pain and abandonment. But eventually I would find so much joy and love. And even as I continue my path toward healing from the choices both you and my mother made concerning me, I am also grateful that God chose to use you to participate in my arrival into this world. Because you, without even knowing it, gave me the gift of your family, and they have given me more love together than you could possibly have mustered on your own. And for that, I am appreciative. I could say soooo much more, but I will leave this letter with a heartfelt, Thank you, Terry.
Your daughter,
Corawana "Candie" A. Mitchell-Price
November 5, 2021

My father, Terry, with a guest, his parents, Evangeline, and John Mitchell.

What are the odds that I would later wear my hair just like he wore his?

Seeing my face in my father's face is a gift that I can't even describe.

STRAIGHT OUTTA BROKENNESS

I am learning!

I am learning. I am learning to love more and more the skin I'm in, the age I am and the YOUniqueness that makes me "ME." I am learning to accept every wrinkle and every imperfection as a badge of honor because they reveal where I've been, what I've been through and where I'm going. Yes, I've been bruised but I'm not broken nor bitter.

I am learning that each day I've been given is a blessing and a do-over - I can continue to walk in the destiny given to me by my Father as He continuously gives me grace to do so.

I am learning that every smile does not equal support, every "like" does not equal love and every tongue does not mean me well. However, I am created in the very image of THE Almighty, sovereign God and His smile, His like and His tongue are all I need to push out my purpose, catapult my gifts and encourage someone else to soar above their circumstances.

I've been there - I've overcome the abandonment and drug abuse of absent parents and family, I've soared past the expectations and statistics of man, and I'm still standing!

I am learning to be open to His Spirit, quiet in His presence and humbled by His grace. I am learning to love ME!

Until that last breath, until these eyes close, I will continue to learn, listen and LEAD!

No matter what YOU are going through keep learning to love God, yourself and others!

c/2015 Candie A. Mitchell-Price

ACKNOWLEDGEMENTS

This book has been a long time in the making, and I owe its completion to so many incredible people who kept me on track! First and foremost, to my wonderful husband, Rev. Arthur Price, Jr., aka The Dude, I am beyond blessed to have you as my biggest cheerleader. Your constant encouragement and belief in my potential mean the world to me. Thank you for teaching me what unconditional love feels like in human form!

To my amazing girls, Eboni and Amyna, thank you for always ensuring I took care of my mental and spiritual health. Your support has been invaluable. I am deeply apologetic for any brokenness that has seeped into your life because of me. I am also 100% accountable for it. Thank you for loving me in spite of it.

I am incredibly grateful for my village of amazing women who rallied around me, especially during the toughest moments of this project. Angela Abdur-Rasheed, your belief in me is invaluable, thanks for all of your help in pushing this project and praying for me!

The Village: (Kim S., Lucretia, Tracie, Glenda, Christie, Lisa, Doella, Kim R., Roberta, Asya, Rindia, and Sha), Veda, and Sister G, each of you has been a source of encouragement and support in so many ways. I am forever grateful. Consuelo, thanks for praying with me and holding me accountable. Your empathy will never be forgotten.

A special shoutout to my godsister, Timyka. Thank you for always being there to listen when I needed it the most.

April Betner, I can't thank you enough for the Zoom calls, inbox messages, and emergency phone calls during some very challenging times. Your wisdom and advice helped guide me toward healing and finding my voice.

To the original WORD GIRL, Martina Lambert, thank you for your spiritual example of what it means to live out the Word of God! The rest of us #wordgirls will forever be grateful for all you've poured into us!

Lastly, but DEFINITELY not least, to the Mitchell family, thank you from the bottom of my heart! You have welcomed, nurtured, and supported me over the past three years, creating a safe space, and an additional village that I now proudly call family. Thank you for welcoming me HOME.

ABOUT THE AUTHOR

A proud native of Philadelphia, PA, Candie has authored two other books, First Lady: The Real Truth and He Restoreth My Soul. She is the Founder and Editor-in-Chief of WOW! (Women of the Word) Magazine, a national lifestyle magazine for Christian women which is returning in January, 2025 (wowmagazine.org). Candie recently launched Word Girlz, a 501c3 dedicated to creating platforms that inspire, encourage, empower, and educate women and girls through the transformative power of the written word.

Candie holds a BA in Communications Studies, specializing in Public Relations, and Master's degrees in Christian Education and Public Relations. A sought-after speaker, she has delivered talks at local and national women's retreats, conferences, and workshops.

She is married to Rev. Arthur Price, Jr., pastor of the historic 16th Street Baptist Church in Birmingham, AL. They are the proud parents of two adult children, Eboni Paige and Amyna Janel.